LIFE IN LINCOLN'S AMERICA

HELEN REEDER CROSS

RANDOM HOUSE

Acknowledgments

The publishers would like to express their gratitude to the following individuals who were particularly helpful during the preparation of this book:

Charles Halgren for advice on trading posts and guns: Miss Geraldine Beard and Miss Shirley Beresford of the New-York Historical Society; Gerald Carson; and Robert Riley for advice on costume.

We would also like to thank the following institutions for their cooperation:

Circus World Museum, Baraboo, Wisconsin; Colonial Williamsburg; Connecticut State Library; Gun Museum, New Haven, Connecticut; Mariners Museum, Newport News, Virginia; Missouri Historical Society; Museum of the City of New York; Museum of the Fur Trade, Chadron, Nebraska; Historical Society of York County, York, Pennsylvania; and the Ringling Circus Museum.

Published in New York by Random House, Inc., and simultaneously in Toronto, Canada, by Random House of Canada, Ltd.

PLANNED AND PRODUCED BY CHANTICLEER PRESS, INC., NEW YORK

Library of Congress Catalog Card Number 64: 20867
Manufactured in the United States of America

Contents

More Than a Hundred Years Ago

Have you ever wondered what daily life was like in America a century and a half ago? Have you ever thought of how people traveled, whether they really ate apple pie for breakfast, and what they did for amusement before movies and television were invented?

In 1800, ours was still a new nation. Not half so large as it is now, it was growing apace, as though trying to stretch itself from the Atlantic to the Pacific. Buffaloes roamed the Western Plains in great herds, Lewis and Clark were tracking their way across unknown mountain and prairie, and twice a year the sky was darkened by the flight of the now-extinct passenger pigeons.

Our cities were scarcely more than sprawling villages. Pigs and chickens roamed streets that were dusty in summer, frozen and full of ruts in winter. Fences of split rails were being laid by lanky young men. Butter was being churned by the daughter or the hired girl of the family. Children, if they were among the lucky ones, went to "blab schools," so-called because you could hear the pupils half a street away as they chanted their ABC's. Panthers and wolves still prowled in the forest. Since there were few bridges, rivers were forded on horseback or crossed by ferryboat, and much of the country still belonged to the Indians, some of whom were friendly, some not.

By 1850, after what had seemed a short half-century, much had changed. Such cities as New York and Pittsburgh had mushroomed. "Spinning factories" for wool and cotton cloth had replaced the fireside spinning wheel. Steamboats were chugging on lake and river. Conestoga wagon trains had forced their way to the Pacific. The miraculous "Iron Horse" was racing twenty to thirty miles an hour along miles of newly-laid rails. It was not an "age of speed" as we know it, but for the Americans of the time it was breath-taking.

If there were some way we might turn back the years and live for a few days in the nineteenth century, whose life would we choose as most typical? We might take someone who knew what it was like to sleep under the roofbeams of a wilderness cabin, with snow sifting down on him through the chinks. Or at the other extreme, it might be someone who knew what it was like to dance in an elegant drawing room lighted by chandeliers with hundreds of shimmering candles.

There were some lives of course that somehow managed to sample almost every kind of experience offered by the America of those years. One such life was that of a man who has born in 1809 and died in 1865—

Clad in wolf skins, Indians hunt buffaloes on the western prairies.

Abraham Lincoln. Beginning life in a one-room cabin, son of a pioneer, Lincoln spent his last years in the White House. Abe Lincoln, whose hands knew the hard work of a poor country boy, whose skin had itched under the roughness of his mother's homespun, later wore fine linen shirts with jet buttons set in silver. He who had practiced writing his alphabet with a piece of charcoal on a fire shovel, later wrote with a fine quill pen on parchment documents. "Honest Abe," who had trudged countless miles on foot and on horseback as a country lawyer, was carried, when he died, in that mechanical marvel, a Pullman car.

Lincoln's life was certainly not typical. Yet astonishing changes like some of these did occur in the lives of all Americans who lived during the first years of the nineteenth century. Many a baby who journeyed west across the plains by prairie schooner or around Cape Horn by clipper ship lived to return by railroad train or newfangled steamboat. Whereas he may have spent his boyhood evenings helping his father cobble shoes for the family, by candlelight, he might well thirty years later have spent his evenings reading a city newspaper by the flame of a gas lamp. Never before in America's history had so much happened to the way people lived, and with such speed. The nineteenth century was an exciting time to be alive.

Frontier Life

I

On the American frontier, the "bornin' " cabin of most pioneer girls and boys, such as Abe Lincoln, was built of logs. These logs, from the very trees cut down to make a clearing, were the most available building material in the wilderness. It took about forty such logs, each twenty to thirty feet long, to construct the usual cabin. The ends were notched and each fitted into the next one in exactly the way pieces of a child's set of "Lincoln logs" build up into a toy cabin. Clay, if any could be found nearby, was used for mortar; but this had a tendency to crumble when dry, often leaving chinks between the logs through which the wind sometimes blew.

Building a cabin was work for a strong man. If a builder had a neighbor not too far off, or a half-grown son to help him, he was lucky. Two men, keeping hard at it, could erect a one-room cabin, roof it, and set its chimney in four or five days, and without a nail in the whole house. Lacking help, a man was likely to house his family in an exposed "half-face lean-to" of tree branches set into a hillside until he could finish their cabin.

Most houses had one cut-out opening with a door hung on leather hinges and one small window without glass. On stormy days, when its wooden shutter was closed, no light crept into the cabin except for the little that came through the chinks between the logs. With that light also came cold wind and rain. A chimney was built into one end of the cabin, its log sides plastered with thick clay.

The "chimbley piece" was the warm heart of every pioneer home. Around its fire the family huddled to dress and undress. Here, during long winter evenings, girls and their mothers knitted by flickering firelight the thick woolen stockings worn by the family. Here boys, when still very young, learned to whittle rough stool and bench legs for new furniture, perhaps wall pegs on which to hang the family's clothes, or bean poles for the garden patch. Here the mother kept a hanging kettle of simmering stew that bubbled and chunked all day over the fire and was eaten from wooden bowls with tin or pewter spoons. Because the chimney was never allowed to grow cold, the whole family could sleep together on the floor when a chance traveler came, all sharing the same scarce bedclothes and all stretching their feet toward the fire for warmth.

To finish his fence the pioneer felled a giant tree and drove wedges into the trunk to split it into rails.

The bed, usually made of poles, was cleated into one corner of the room. Probably there was a mattress of harsh corn husks. Only a few log cabin families had hen-feather beds. For cover there might be a bearskin. Cabins sometimes had a second bed in a corner for the children, and a low trundle bed might be trundled under the big one in the daytime. If a wilderness father was clever at carpentry he made a cradle for the newest baby. Then its mother could rock the tiny one with her foot while her hands were busy at spinning or sewing, shelling beans, or stringing onions to hang from the rafters.

Many pioneers were wanderers, forever seeking a plot of richer land—a life that might be, but seldom was, a bit easier. In the early part of the nineteenth century the Middle West was called the "Ohio Country." It was then a wilderness-covered, lonesome land, with the nearest neighbors miles away. Indiana was a place where, one writer said, "the panther's scream filled night with fear," where "bears preyed on the swine." It was a hard way to live, typical of the shifting life of many pioneer families on the western frontier.

Building each new cabin was much like building the last one. Clearing stubborn rocks to make a "truck patch" for cabbages and beans and radishes, for corn and potatoes and onions, was backbreaking work. A child had scarcely learned to walk before the help of his small hands was asked: to run errands, to fetch water perhaps a mile from the spring, to weed the garden and carry wood, to pick up wild-grown windfall crab apples.

Planting, Rail Splitting, and Beautifying

At planting time, a father or older brother would walk ahead in "the big field." A small boy trailed behind, dropping grains of corn into hills. Two pumpkin seeds also went into every other hill, every other row, as the Indians had taught the early settlers.

When a boy grew older, his tasks grew harder. There were the horses and cows, perhaps a pig to care for, logs to cut and split, fences to mend and to build, a floor of "slabs" to lay for a fancier cabin, plowing to be done, and a "lucky-year" or bumper harvest to get in—if wind and bad weather, marauding beasts, or Indians did not strike the little clearing.

For most pioneer boys there was always the excitement of hunting. Once when his father was away from home, seven-year-old Abe Lincoln, like many another pioneer boy, saw a flock of wild turkeys flying overhead. He rushed for the rifle that hung on a pair of buck's horns beside the cabin door. Then he aimed and shot at the birds through a chink in the wall. A turkey fell to earth, dead. That day there was boiled

Early settlers were resourceful fence-makers. Top to bottom: a snake fence, a post-and-rail, and a solid zig-zag.

A good day's hunting means furs for the trading post and meat for the stew pot.

turkey for dinner. Other days, for many pioneer families, the main dish might be venison steak, squirrel or rabbit stew.

Meanwhile, the girls of the house were learning a woman's work. This meant the many tasks of keeping a home, but with no labor-saving aids: a fire to keep burning; spinning and weaving, if the family had a spinning wheel and loom; a cow to milk; the garden to hoe; bugs to pick from tender leaves; and soap to make in an outdoor kettle. And there was the eternal knitting, as well as sewing heavy buckskins into shirts and trousers for the menfolk.

This last could be made to satisfy a girl's love of "purty" things. She could fringe her father's hunting jacket and sew beads on his moccasins as she had seen Indian women do. But such "foolishness" took time, and time was something there was too little of, for a pioneer girl's work was never finished.

When life itself is hard, that which is useful must come before that which is ornamental. But even in the early days of nation-building, men and women tried to supply a little charm in their homes in many different ways: wild flowers were tucked into the chinks in the cabin walls; fresh, sweet-smelling grass was mixed with mint and strewn on the puncheon floor when company was expected; linsey-woolsey was dyed a soft red with pokeberry juice, or blue with wild indigo, before it was used for a girl's new shift; and a mantel shelf was built over the fireplace so that the family's prized pewter plates would gleam in the firelight.

Death knocked often on the door of pioneer cabins. Because doctors did not live near at hand, there were only old wives' tales and Indian remedies to be tried desperately in an emergency: pipsissewa leaves, boneset tea, a tonic of snake's head, or wild cherry bark. But none of these could save Nancy Hanks Lincoln when she was taken with the "milk sickness," thought to have been caused by the milk of a cow that had eaten poisonous plants.

So for a hard and lonely year Abe and his sister Sarah kept house for their father, until he returned to Kentucky and brought back a stepmother for them—a widow, her name also Sarah. She brought with her a wagon-load of the first real furniture Abe and his sister had ever seen: bedsteads, a bureau with drawers, a polished table and chairs, a feather mattress and pillows. She also brought three children of her own, and ways of making a home seem warm and good.

But the one-room cabin was now crowded. It was time for the bigger boys to climb the ladder and sleep in the loft under the sloping roof beams. This was the usual lot of older sons when new babies crowded the one-room cabin. Here Abe could lie and watch stars twinkle through the cracks; here he awakened on many a winter morning to find snow on his eyelashes. Rarely did the sun coming through those chinks get a chance to wake the boys. For they arose long "afore sun-up" to do the chores. Down the ladder they came—faster no doubt in cold weather—and in front of the fire pulled their clothes on over the underwear in which they had slept. Every boy wore buckskin breeches, tow sack shirt with perhaps a leather jacket for hunting, and a coonskin cap, tail hanging behind.

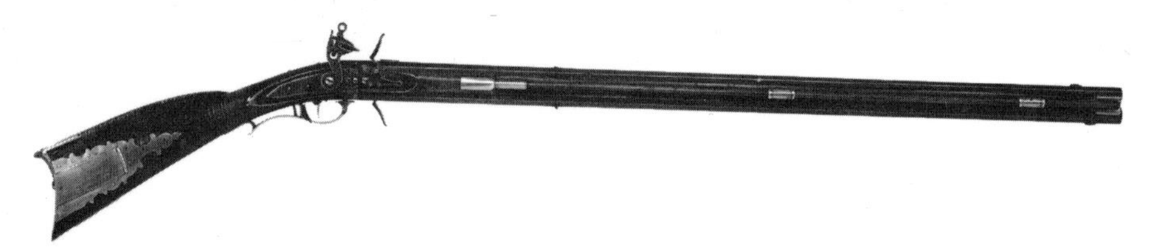

Many pioneers carried a Kentucky flintlock rifle (above) but by mid-century the "plains rifle" (left) was in common use.

Girls slipped loose, sad-colored linsey-woolsey dresses over their heads and were dressed for the day. When out-of-doors in summer they wore sunbonnets; in winter, hooded capes or shawls. In summer everybody went barefoot; in winter they wore the heavy woolen stockings that womenfolk spent their spare time knitting the year round. Sometimes men and women tied on strips of birch bark over their socks and wound bands of deerskin, like leggings, from ankle to knee. Only a few pioneers were clever enough to cobble shoes from deerskin; fewer still had money enough to buy footgear from the storekeeper in the nearest settlement.

Fording the river Platte at high water could mean flooding the wagons and doing damage to precious possessions.

Frontier Food and Hospitality

A usual breakfast was either the mush or stew that had simmered all night while the family slept, or corn dodgers baked in hot coals. There were milk and butter for those families lucky enough to have a cow. The Southern log cabin family might also enjoy molasses made from its own sugar cane. Northerners, if lucky, sometimes smoked out a bee tree and reveled in the stolen honey.

Though life in a frontier cabin was certainly hard, most families, even those who had set out for wilderness life with fewest possessions, ate well, especially if the father was a hunter or a fisherman. Vegetables were often stored in a hole under the floor boards of the cabin. Some vegetables—such as onions, turnips, potatoes, peppers, and pumpkin slices—were hung to dry from the rafters, ready at hand for the stew pot. In season there were berries and nuts to be had for the picking. There was "sass"—greens of various kinds—from the vegetable patch, and, in southern climes, a bit of tobacco for father. In the leanest months of winter a smoked, dried haunch of last year's venison, called "jerk," could be stewed to some degree of tenderness. The settler who trapped or hunted for furs often made money; with this he could buy chickens and pigs at the nearest settlement. Then, indeed, his family ate richly—unless wolves, Indians, a bear, or a gap in the fence deprived him of his prizes.

Thus the American tradition of pioneer hospitality began with food. The lone traveler was very welcome in the log cabin of the news-hungry settler and his family. No one ever asked for a stranger's pedigree or credentials. He was pressed to stay for a visit, to tell what was happening in the world "back home" in New England, or Pennsylvania, or the tidewater Carolinas. Instead of being embarrassed at the crudeness of the rough stools and table, the bench and shelves hacked into some kind of shape by his own unskilled hand, the pioneer shared what he had with pride—especially his food. And there was usually much to be proud of. After all, none of it—except salt, an occasional spice, and coffee—had been bought over the counter of a store.

For daily living, too, the wilderness family made everything it needed except needles, thread, an ax, and a rifle. These people took pride in being able to manage almost entirely by themselves. The supreme essential for pioneer life was a good water supply. A clear, gushing spring was ideal. Most cabin sites were chosen with this in mind. Many a village and city in today's America got its name—Sweetwater or Springfield, Warm Springs or Spring Valley—from a stream joyfully found there by its first settler. Thomas Lincoln during his hard lifetime dug three different wells to supply his family with water. In this, as in many things, such as land titles that seemed never to be clear, he was unlucky: each of the three Lincoln wells sooner or later went dry in a rainless season.

A Green Wilderness Tamed

Most wilderness families did not stay in one place long enough to see civilization gain a foothold there. But often the frontier family that had found a good water supply and fertile soil—and perhaps a broad stream

Gamblers often did their talking with guns.

Early photograph of Main Street, Helena, Montana, a typical Western town in the 1860's.

on which to float produce to the nearest trading post—before long found itself attracting neighbors. This often happened in the rich country of the Middle West. Once the wilderness spell had been broken, other roving families settled near-by.

At first they came single file, then in waves. In Ohio, Indiana, Illinois, and Missouri, between 1820 and 1840, these new settlers proceeded to burn stumps, and to build fences, barns, roads and bridges. They planted orchards, built grist and sawmills and practiced crafts. Groups of neighboring farmers would decide that it was high time to erect a church, then a schoolhouse. Businessmen drifted into the new settlement and set up a primitive trading post which later became a well-stocked store. Almost without realizing it, the new community became a thriving town. By 1840, there were more people living in beautiful, fertile Ohio than in Massachusetts. The Middle West was no longer an outpost of civilization, but a vigorous, settled part of the nation.

But many still continued to press westward. A determined pioneer would have found it hard to express in words his reasons for choosing so hard, lonely, and unsettled a life for himself and his family. They might

Work begins in earnest for women when wagons are "coiled" for the night.

include the search for fertile acres all his own, for a never-failing spring of water, or for space uncluttered with other people. Some men sought escape from religious oppression. This was especially true of the Mormons who settled what is now the State of Utah. Others were trying to escape the long arm of the law. Many mountain men or fur trappers, displaying "a wild and ferocious kinship with the animals they stalked," were of this kind. Still others were impelled by the lure of the unknown, by some force stronger than common sense.

It seems incredible that America, as late as 1830, was settled only halfway across the continent. Independence, Missouri, was the "jumping-off place"—the last "civilized" town with stores, schools, churches, neighbors just behind a picket fence, and a feeling of safety when night fell. Beyond Independence lay fifteen hundred miles of almost unknown country. Even those most eager to try a new life in a new land were intimidated by tales that had filtered back East of vast distances, unscalable mountain ranges, and Indian trouble. Yet westward they continued to press; at first slowly, then with gathering momentum. There is a story that the famous orator, Henry Clay, paused while passing through the Cumberland Gap. When asked why, he replied, "I am listening to the tread of the coming millions."

Western Fever

The contagion of this "Western" or "Oregon Fever" swept the country, striking solid citizens as well as adventurers. Whole communities devel-

Travel across the dusty plains was thirsty work.

oped the fever simultaneously: the coastal farmer whose land was "played out" (land that even at its best had been "a-bilin'" with rocks) and the underpaid mill hands and clerks of village and city. By the thousands, farmers sold their land for whatever it would bring in a market already flooded with poor farmland. They herded their livestock, piled their families, belongings, and pets into wagons drawn by horses, oxen, or mules, and set forth for the Promised Land.

The invention of the Conestoga Wagon, named for the Pennsylvania town where it was first made, encouraged the move west. It was a hardy vehicle, made from seasoned timber reinforced with iron. Strong hoops were arched across the wagon body, and stretched over these was the canvas cover familiar to every moviegoer. Smaller covered wagons were given the picturesque name of "prairie schooners."

Inside, a wagon was packed with every kind of provision the emigrant family might need for its new life in the Golden West. They bought the best guns and ammunition they could afford. They took clothes, tinware, furniture, blankets, farm implements, and crop seeds. For the journey itself they packed tents, corned beef, parched corn, dried apples, pumpkin, and potatoes, as well as jerk (strips of dried beef or venison) and pemmican (dried buffalo meat). Some families, lacking money, were pitifully supplied; others had every necessity, even luxuries. Most women took young apple and pear trees, a lilac and a rosebush, and roots of medicinal herbs. These they watered painstakingly, even when they themselves were thirsty.

Above: Early pistol of the Kentucky flintlock type. Below: Brass pipe tomahawk, 1860.

On the Trail

The usual wagon train was made up of all kinds of men: the sober and industrious, the lazy and incompetent, the God-fearing and the untrustworthy. Only the foolhardy family undertook the trip alone. Many young men without money, as well as adventurers seeking an easy fortune, joined a caravan with the understanding that they would work their way across the country. These were put to driving teams, herding livestock or acting as scouts.

Family wagons made their separate ways to meeting points like St. Louis or Independence, Missouri. Along the National Road and the Wilderness Trail they poured. Some put their wagons on flatboats and floated down the Wabash or the Ohio rivers to the starting place of the next caravan. Fifty or sixty wagons were considered a good number for safety's sake, though many trains had more than a hundred. Most caravans set out in May, while the prairies were green with grass not yet high enough to become lost in. With much luck, such a wagon train might hope to spend Thanksgiving on the beautiful Columbia River in what is now the State of Washington, but was then known as the "Oregon Country."

Before setting out, the men of the caravan formed a loose society—with leaders, scouts, and a system of rules agreed to by all—for, once west

Indian attacks were a constant peril to the immigrants.

of Missouri, they would be beyond the protection of the United States. A strict discipline had to be kept. Mealtimes, startings hours, corralling of livestock—all must move like clockwork. The slowpoke wagon was ordered to the rear of the column, there to choke on dust all day. Ordinarily, a family had to endure a rear position only when its turn came.

The advance was slow at best. Travelers might choose to stay in the uncomfortable, springless wagon, or, for a change, they might prefer to walk or ride horseback. There was time for a woman to pick the strange and lovely prairie flowers, to rock the baby, play games with the children, or knit and sew. When the weather behaved, it was a beautiful prairie. Late in the day, the leader called a halt— near a spring or waterhole if he could find one—and like a slow, practiced dance movement, the wagons would describe a huge circle. Each wagon tongue was chained to the rear of the vehicle before it, for this magic circle meant safety—protection from Indians or wolf pack. Horses, oxen, and cows were allowed to graze outside the circle until darkness. Then they were hobbled, and a watch set over them. If danger was suspected, they were driven inside the circle.

All our western movies and stories tell of the pioneer's fear of Indians. But who among us stops to think of what the red man must have thought of the strangers who invaded his plains? There is a true Indian tale of a Paiute hunting party; as it crossed the plains the band

. . . was surprised to see a vast cloud of dust, far different from the usual desert whirlwind. Cautiously watching from the protection of high sagebrush and rocks, they were astonished to see that the cloud moved, and horrified to discover it was "following them."

Panic-stricken, they bolted through the brush, but the cloud still followed. Luckily it stopped at dusk, and as the Paiute hunters watched, they saw a long, moving white object crawl into a coil, and stop.

Evening, when the caravan had "coiled," was the time for women to bestir themselves. Since early morning, if there had been no trouble, their hours had been freer by far than those back at home. Now cooking and watch fires must be hastily built of cottonwood and "chips" of buffalo dung. Cows must be milked, supper cooked, clothes and children washed in a near-by stream, and bedding unrolled and laid on the ground or inside tents. Now children could exercise freely. Teamsters could relax. There might be singing and storytelling with harmonica or accordion music beside the fire. But even on the best of days, bones and muscles were weary. Soon the caravan slept—that is, all except the "watch." If he so much as dozed, he would be made to walk beside his horse all next day as penalty. It was imperative for the safety of the wagon train that this one man stay alert; his ears had to be attuned to the howl of hyena or wolf, hoot of owl, or screech of wildcat, for any of these cries might, in reality, be an Indian signal.

Trials and Tragedies

All this may sound like a pleasant if rather strenuous camping trip spent with friends. No doubt most caravans enjoyed some good days, but all was not usually so calm and well-ordered. Even for those fortunate few who had a fairly easy trek west, there were almost unbearable daily trials.

A gold miner's life held many surprises.

Francis Parkman, a young Easterner just out of Yale University who was later to become a famous historian, made the trip on the "Oregon Trail." In 1846 this meant an arduous journey from St. Louis across Kansas and Nebraska to Fort Laramie, in Wyoming. In his book called *The Oregon Trail,* Parkman listed a few minor annoyances that could dampen the ardor of the most eager explorer:

His wagons will stick in the mud; his horse will break loose; harness will give way; and axle-trees prove unsound. His bed will be a soft one, consisting often of black mud of the richest consistency. As for food, he must content himself with biscuit and salt provisions . . . He will find himself beset with "varmints" innumerable. The wolves will entertain him with a concert at night, and skulk around him by day, just beyond rifle shot; his

Shooting buffalo from trains was a favorite sport of the 1860's.

> *horse will step into badger holes; from every marsh and mud-puddle will arise the bellowing, croaking and trilling of legions of frogs . . . A profusion of snakes will glide away from under his horse's feet, or quietly visit him in his tent at night; while the pertinacious humming of unnumbered mosquitoes will banish sleep from his eyelids. When thirsty with a long ride in the scorching sun over some boundless reach of prairie, he comes at length to a pool of water, and alights to drink, he discovers a troop of young tadpoles sporting in the bottom of his cup.*

The wild animals that the pioneers met were perhaps equally divided between the welcome and the unwelcome. A geography book written in 1806 describes the bison or wild ox, which the author warns his readers not to misname "buffalo," and the red and fallow deer; there was also the bear, which is "very fond of sweet, vegetable food such as sweet apples, Indian corn in the milk, berries, grapes, honey," and which "frequently destroys calves, sheep, pigs and sometimes children." He goes on to give a fearful description of the wolf, and of the catamount, cougar, mountain cat, and lynx. Lastly, he names thirty-seven varieties of snakes, some deadly, others harmless.

Then there was the weather. The Great Plains suffered summers of searing heat, interrupted by fierce thunderstorms of rain, wind, and hail. Winters were long, bitter, and deep with snow.

Both Charles Dickens and Parkman tell of seeing hastily erected wooden crosses which marked the graves of young and old alike—those whose constitutions had not been strong enough to bear the trials of the migration. They also tell of seeing castoff bedsteads, bureaus, trunks—once lovingly rubbed and prized, now decaying beside the trail. These had been discarded to lighten a load for an exhausted team, or make it possible for a wagon to push on through mud or snowdrift.

In desert regions there were sandstorms to blind and choke the travelers. There were prairie fires, runaway horses, clouds of grasshoppers, lost trails, and sickness. There was water made undrinkable by alkali deposits; grass too scant for grazing; rivers too swollen to ford, and possessions water-logged and ruined. Most of all, there were buffaloes and Indians—sometimes to be welcomed and sometimes to be feared.

No wonder rueful verses were composed to sing to familiar tunes, such as this one to "Beulah Land":

We've reached the land of desert sweet,
Where nothing grows for man to eat.
The wind it blows with feverish heat
Across the plains so hard to beat.

Using rope lariats, early settlers lassoed the wild horses that roamed the prairies.

We've reached the land of hills and stones
Where all is strewn with buffalo bones.
O buffalo bones, bleached buffalo bones,
I seem to hear your sighs and moans.

Of all the chronicles of the westward push, the most tragic is that of the Donner party. The Donner and Reed families had set out with high hopes, for they were well equipped with money and supplies. When they left Missouri, there were more than two hundred wagons in the train.

All went well until the caravan reached Wyoming. At this point, the Donner group ventured upon a little-known short cut, the Hastings cutoff. This was a tragic mistake, for it led the travelers straight across the barren, trackless desert beyond Salt Lake. Violent quarrels among some of the leaders added to the general misery, but worse was to come. The pioneers lingered too long in the high Sierra Nevada mountains which separate Nevada from California, and early snows caught them there. In what is still known as "Donner Pass," they were marooned throughout a long, bitter winter. Only half the emigrants survived. A diary kept by one of the party tells the gruesome story of how some of them were driven by near-starvation to eat the flesh of those who died.

Prospecting for gold in an icy stream of the Far West.

Red Man and Buffalo

The Indian struck fear into the hearts of wagon train emigrants. Only a few white men realized, with Lieutenant John C. Fremont, explorer and friend of Kit Carson, that the "Indians and buffalo make the poetry and life of the prairie." Even Fremont himself killed both freely whenever the occasion arose. Few explorers and settlers remembered that the West really belonged to the Red Man. In Indian eyes it was the gift of the "Great Spirit." This was his home; the white man was the intruder. The relentless way in which white Americans pushed tribe after tribe from its ancestral home all across the continent is a dark chapter in our history. And we did not stop until both Indian and buffalo were almost destroyed.

Most of us have seen a buffalo or two in a zoo. It is hard to realize that not so many years ago these lumbering animals roamed the Western Plains in great herds. In *The Oregon Trail,* Parkman describes plains speckled as far as the eye could see with herds of buffalo. Bulls, cows, and calves scattered before the horses of the intruding white man. A lone bull, startled while grazing, would leap up when surprised, stare stupidly at the intruder, then gallop clumsily away.

The buffalo represented many things to both Indian and white. Its flesh was steak and roast, stew and pemmican; its hide could be scraped and made into a tent, or left hairy for warmth as rug or robe. It was also exciting to hunt. Pitting one's prowess against a startled herd of buffalo, which might at any moment unhorse the hunter and trample him underfoot, was thrilling to the sportsman. Untold thousands of the great beasts

Miners enjoying a Thanksgiving Dinner in their cabin.

were killed for the sake of sport, their skeletons left to bleach upon the plains in wanton wastefulness. Fremont thus describes a buffalo hunt in his Report:

> *As we were riding quietly along the bank, a grand herd of buffalo, some seven or eight hundred in number, came crowding up the river, where they had been to drink, and commenced crossing the plain slowly, eating as they went. The wind was favorable; the coolness of the morning invited to exercise . . . and the distance across the prairie (two or three miles) gave us a fine opportunity to charge them before they could get among the river hills . . .*
>
> *In a few moments . . . we were going over the ground like a hurricane. When at about thirty yards, we gave the usual shout (the hunter's battle cry) and broke into the herd . . . the mass*

Prospecting for gold was not a job for weaklings.

> *giving way in every direction in their heedless course. Many of the bulls, less active and less fleet than the cows . . . were precipitated to the earth with great force, rolling over and over with the violence of the shock, and hardly distinguishable in the dust.*

Only a few men with prophetic vision dreamed with Parkman more than a hundred years ago:

> *. . . that a time would come when these plains would be a grazing country, the buffalo give place to tame cattle, farmhouses be scattered along the watercourses, and wolves, bears, and Indians be numbered among the things that were.*

Gold Fever

If Western Fever was a disease, the Gold Fever of 1849 was like a plague. Thousands of citizens of previously sane minds and sensible habits seemed to go mad. Many lost their lives because of it; others lost the fortunes they began with; a few became fabulously rich overnight, only to lose all in a twinkling because of land speculation or gambling.

The bright yellow metal was discovered in the race of a sawmill owned by Johann A. Sutter in the Sacramento Valley. When word of the find reached the East, thousands of adventurers set out pell-mell for the gold fields. They poured across the Great Plains and the Rockies, across the Gila Trail from Texas to California, or by ship around Cape Horn. Few took the time to prepare adequately for the journey. Many turned back—discouraged by mountain peaks, desert heat, or Indian trouble—without ever reaching the gold fields. An observer estimated that fewer than one in twenty returned home in as good pocket as when he set out. One of the few women living at a mining camp put the matter neatly. She wrote in her diary, "Gold mining is Nature's great lottery scheme."

Not all fortunes were made by discovering gold. Many were made by merchants or others who gouged the miners with outrageous prices. One fortune-seeker wrote of a lady who "cooked and sold from early morn to dewy eve dried apple pies for five dollars each . . . a short twelve months could turn her out a millionaire." Gold dust and nuggets were in careless circulation up and down the West Coast. One miner, desperate for shoes, offered fifty dollars for a pair. Needles sold for a dollar each.

Many miners died of exposure, for the digging was done in canyon gulches flowing with icy water. Shelters at the camps were crude and inadequate. To these trials were added all the old dangers of hostile Indians and wild animals.

San Francisco was a bonanza town. Here boatload after boatload of hopeful gold miners docked after their long voyage around Cape Horn. The town burst overnight from a quiet fishing village into a ramshackle city, sprawling out and becoming dirty, overcrowded and hazardous. There was constant danger of fire in the flimsy buildings. Law enforcement was scant. Gambling houses and saloons never shut their doors. It was a flamboyant life in a raw, new part of America—a hard place for a woman to make a decent home, and a harder place in which to grow up. There were no schools, no churches, and few men whose lives were worth taking as models. It must have been far from easy for a mid-nineteenth century son or daughter of a gold-fever victim to grow up with anything but a grab-as-grab-can, get-rich-quick aim in life. Fortunately, there were few children in the Gold Rush towns during their wildest days. Yet, as we know, the Far West has developed into as law-abiding and stable an area as any other in the United States.

Northern Farm and Southern Plantation

2

Although many families went west, countless others clung to the farms which had belonged to their fathers. Nothing could tear them from the acres which they and their families had so recently fought and died for in the American Revolution. The well-tilled fields and the New England saltbox or the plantation farmhouse in which their families had lived for two, three, or four generations were "home." Here they would stay and bring up their children, like their fathers before them.

Sometimes the farmhouse was built of stone, sometimes of clapboard painted ochre or barn red or white. It was often two stories high, with lean-tos and extra rooms added as the family grew. There was a vine-shaded well-house near the kitchen door, perhaps a smokehouse, and a garden of hollyhock, sunflowers, hundred-leaf roses, clove pinks, and a snowball bush. Almost always in the North a pair of lilac bushes flanked the front stoop. In the South the farmhouse, sometimes with stately Grecian pillars on its verandah, was set far back from the road, with an avenue bordered with poplar, elm, or blossoming crape myrtle trees leading to the door. Every farm had its orchard of apple, pear or plum trees. In the South there were peach and pecan, too.

In Vermont, Maine, and New Hampshire, there were barns for the livestock. These were sometimes attached to the kitchen end of the house so that the family would not have to go out in bad weather to tend the animals. Often the barn was much larger than the farmhouse itself; for livestock—cows, horses, pigs, sheep and chickens—were a valuable part of the farmer's property and must be treated with every care.

Johnny Cake and Plum Flummery

In many ways the farm home was as independent as the log cabin. In winter the family kept itself warm and comfortable with fireplace fires. As late as 1831 there were no friction matches; fires were started by striking flint and steel together over a tin box full of lint. Once a blaze was going well, it was fed by wood that father and sons had chopped from their own timberland and kept stored in the woodshed behind the kitchen. Many farm families still cooked over this fire. Hearths had Dutch ovens built into brick or stone chimneys. Red-hot coals were shovelled into these, then removed when the oven was hot enough for baking. Here Johnny cake (or what we call cornbread), loaves of fragrant "rye and Injun"

The overseer talks business as slaves bring cotton to the new gin.

bread, mincemeat pie, and Boston beans were baked every Saturday.

The smokehouse ceiling was hung thickly with hams and sides of bacon. The cellar was stocked with potatoes and Mackintosh apples, with onions, carrots, turnips (rutabagas in the South), parsnips, and winter squash. Hanging in the kitchen from the exposed rafters were dried bunches of sage and mint, of rosemary and dill for seasoning soups and stews. There was often a springhouse, or covered enclosure built over the spring which supplied the family with water. Here was a cool, shady spot, even in the summer. Water freshly sprung from deep underground sources was ice cold on the hottest day. Tubs of freshly churned butter and crocks of thick cream were set there, ready for raspberry or plum flummery, a kind of custard which was one of Abe Lincoln's favorite desserts.

They ate like kings, most of these nineteenth century farm families. But unlike the monarchs of history, they ran little risk of developing the gout, which comes from overeating plus an indolent life. For farm work was hard exercise. It burned up many calories. Breakfast on a New Hampshire farm in 1817 is described in the following account written in 1870:

How some of the old settlers could eat. In olden times huge basins of bean-porridge and loaves as big as bee hives . . . and as brown as the backs of their own hands, delighted and refreshed our ancestors. To this fare they would betake themselves with a capacity that only pure air and hard labor can give . . . Christian William Whiteman, who lived on the top of Height-o'-land, said he "could eat three quarts of baked beans and also Indian pudding and other 'fixings' suitable to accompany them at his morning meal." Mr. Pixley, a tall gaunt man who once resided in Charleston by Tarleton Lake, said that "many a time he had eaten a six quart pan full of pork and beans and vinegar, at a single sitting and then could make a famine among the pies and cakes and cheese on the table."

Chores, Chores, Chores

Girls and their mothers, perhaps also a maiden Aunt Sally or Lavinia who lived with the family, sewed patchwork or patterned quilt tops in Rose-of-Sharon, Pine Tree, or Double Wedding Ring patterns, and embroidered their own cambric petticoats. They hemmed unbleached sheets and stuffed mattresses with hen feathers and goose down instead of corn husks, which were scorned by settled folk. In the beginning of the century they dipped candles; later they cleaned the chimneys of whale-oil lamps. Often there was a hired girl to help with the endless round of household tasks.

A farmer and his sons still went hunting whenever they felt a hankering for venison or for wild turkey or pigeon pie. So carelessly were both turkeys and passenger pigeons destroyed by hunters that they have disappeared completely from our woodlands. Today we can only read with wonder about the great flocks of passenger pigeons whose flight once darkened the sky at sunset. Sometimes a farmer and his sons stalked the fox which had raided the henhouse or stolen a lamb. If it was back-

By hand or by ingenious stump-pullers, settlers clear their land for cultivation.

country, there were still wolves and bobcats. And of course they fished near-by streams and lakes for the giant salmon and trout which were so plentiful.

In winter they cut and hauled great blocks of thick ice from the nearest pond to store deep underground in the hillside icehouse where perishable foods were kept in summer. Always there was plowing and sowing, cultivating and harvesting of buckwheat, rye, Indian corn, winter and summer wheat, and, in the South, of sugarcane, rice, tobacco, and cotton. Farm work was hard in those days, as it has been in every land until machines and electricity came.

To help him with his chores, the farmer who could afford it kept a hired man or boy. He gave him board at the family table, a few dollars twice a year, and a cubbyhole room off the kitchen or "up attic." Sometimes, if his farm was large, a farmer would hire several helpers, especially for harvesting. There is one story of a Rev. Samuel Stebbins who had a knack of squeezing prodigious amounts of work from his harvest helpers. Sickles in hand, the men lined up at one end of the field while, watch in hand, Mr. Stebbins gave the signal to begin the work race. Each man was determined "to cut out" the man beside him.

> *"Surprising," said Mr. Stebbins as the men completed the first rush through the grain field. "I don't think you can go through again so quick—but if you think you can, you may try—and I'll hold the watch." Again they set in, and rush across the field and return in less time than before. "Amazing! I didn't think it possible to reap across the field in so short a time. I'm sure you can't do it again—but if you think you can, take a drink of rum, and you may try once more—and I'll hold the watch." They go through with greater speed than before. "Ah, I had not thought you could beat yourselves as you have done. Half a minute less time than before." And thus, under the influence of the Dominie's rum and flattery, a vast amount of work was done.*

Refinements for the Farmhouse

Though Eastern and New England farm life had much in common with that of the log cabin family on America's rough frontier, it did not need to be half so self-sufficient. Furniture did not have to be carved or whittled by hand. Some farmhouses were furnished with lovely highboys, chests and beds with carved pineapple posts. These had come over on ships from the Old Country with long-ago Dutch, English, or German ancestors, or had been brought more recently on a clipper ship by a seafaring son or uncle. Shoes, though still crude and heavy by today's standards, were no longer made by the father of a family, but by a traveling cobbler. Spinning and weaving in the home was also gradually disappearing because of cotton mills. Corn was no longer laboriously ground by hand between two stones, but by water power at the nearest grist mill.

Above: Haystacks took many forms. Below: A field hand sharpens his cradle scythe.

In fact, there was a mill for every imaginable purpose—for making cider, salt, flax, plaster, linseed oil, tobacco, barrel staves, axes, bone meal, mustard and so forth. In one town, within a walk of a minute or two, there were once thirty mills—almost as many as near-by houses. Travelers could tell they were near "civilization" by the steady beat of the "plumping mills."

All sorts of refinements had found their way into the farm home. Curtains hung at glass windowpanes. Doors had hinges of stout brass or wrought iron in fancy shapes. Floors were of painted or waxed hardwood and were decorated with round or oval rugs, hand-braided of brightly dyed rags. In prosperous farm homes, flowered paper covered the walls, and crocheted coverlets were used for "looks," not warmth, on the beds.

Keeping in perfect time, farm hands work their way across a field.

Women and girls cut their dresses from patterns they hoped were stylish and then from the scraps made sunbonnets to match.

All this had happened, of course, because most farms, even if tucked away in the purple folds of hill and mountain, were not too many miles from a village where more and more things could be bought ready-made. One could get plows and scythes, cowhide shoes that almost fit, milk pails and Blue Willow plates, yards of sprigged calico and widow's veiling, and even a red and yellow wooden rocking horse with glass eyes.

Though they were far from good in extremes of weather, roads and turnpikes, instead of a narrow wilderness trail, began to wind their way past many farmhouses. It was a poor farmer who did not own a team of horses and a wagon (perhaps also a buggy or carriage) in which to carry his produce to market and his family to church sociables or Fourth of July celebrations in the nearest village.

County Fairs and Yankee Peddlers

In late summer and autumn there was the County Fair to bring farm folk together in friendly competition. In the early 1800's, a few farseeing farmers realized that American livestock and farming methods needed improving. Farmers organized agricultural societies for pooling their knowledge. Members proudly wore "Wheat Cockades" in their tall hats. The County Fair became the annual showtime for farm products and livestock. Cattle, horses, sheep, pigs and poultry were judged and awarded "premium tags," just as they are today at fairs. The best butter, cheese, jam, and quilts made by farm wives were given blue ribbons and certificates of merit. So were samples of the finest wheat and corn, squash, apples, and pumpkins. To the serious competitions was added the excitement of horse racing, plowing contests, ox-pulling, and, barn dances.

For those farm homes too far from a town for easy coming and going,

Powerful, obedient and durable, oxen served the settlers well.

there was the wonderful institution known as the Yankee peddler, whose visit was an event eagerly anticipated by lonely back-country families.

"Here he comes, Ma!" the brightest-eyed boy would yell from the tree where he was picking apples. Everyone would rush pellmell to door or window to watch the gaily painted wagon come into sight over the hill. Mother and daughters raced to the stoop, half-churned butter forgotten, chickens only half fed, needle left dangling in the quilting frame. Father and boys came in early from the field, pretending to think it time for dinner. This was a rare day.

The peddler's wagon was a clever contraption. Its sides sometimes opened wide and folded back, displaying wares that made everyone's eyes shine: glittering tin pots and pans, fat pocket watches with a loud tick, packets of needles, bolts of bright cloth, umbrellas, "Chiny" tea, cinnamon bark, and spectacles of simple magnifying glass set in gold frames for grandpa's failing eyes.

Boys pulled pennies—saved since Christmas—from their pockets. Now which to buy—wooden top, striped agate, or five anise candy canes, smooth and sweet? Small girls looked hungrily at wax or wooden dolls in red and blue calico dresses with pantalettes showing daintily, like their own. Older sisters had saved for a robin's-egg-blue ribbon to run through a lace collar, or glass buttons to trim a Sunday dress. Ma had saved her egg money for spools of sewing silk, a newfangled rolling pin for biscuit dough, and a coral necklace for the baby, to ward off "shakes and fever," or malaria. The farmer himself wanted his axe and butchering knives sharpened on the peddler's grindstone. He was glad to trade three pounds of his best maple sugar for new rifle shells and a "store-boughten" collar.

Most of all, the whole farm family welcomed the news that the Yankee peddler brought from the outside world. He was a sociable man who loved the attention he received at every stop. Yes, he'd be glad to take dinner with the family, thank ye. Indeed, this gourdful was the sweetest and coldest spring water he'd tasted in many a long day. He hadn't forgotten the lady's cooking from last year. Her apple pandowdy was the best he'd found, and her fried chicken was enough to make a body's mouth water.

After noonday dinner and a nap in the sun on the stoop, the peddler could sometimes be persuaded to tune up his fiddle or his "juice harp" for a bit of music to delight the children. If his visit came at day's end, he told stories of the faraway world of men and cities by firelight until bedtime, then was given the best featherbed as an honored guest for the night.

He was known as a shrewd bargainer, this peddler. But so was the Yankee farmer with whom he traded. It was a game of wits that both seller and buyer played, each wary and eager to get the better of the other. Connecticut is still known as the Nutmeg State because of the wooden nutmegs that some dishonest peddler sold farm women up and down the countryside. If you have ever seen a whole nutmeg, you know that only its smell and taste when licked, or grated over apple sauce distinguishes the spicy nut from its wooden substitute.

The Southern Plantation

There was a world of difference between New England farm life and that of the southern tidewater plantation. The Northern or Bay State farm-

Young and old gather to enjoy a plowing match.

It was hard to resist the Yankee peddler's tempting wares, especially when you lived far from a city or even a village store.

house was built tight and snug, with few windows and low ceilings, in rooms which were small enough to keep warm, each with its own hearth fire. The story-and-a-half saltbox house had a steeply sloping roof in the back, so that snow would slide off quickly. The front door opened into a tiny, unheated entry. The house was built close to street or road, so that long paths need not be shoveled through snow to the hitching post.

For exactly opposite reasons, the plantation home of the Southern large-scale farmer was built with a broad entrance hall, spacious rooms and high ceilings, French doors and many windows, so that air might circulate freely and keep the house as cool as possible during the torrid summer. The mansion was set back from the dust of the road, at the end of a shady avenue of magnolias. On its wide verandah, family and guests rocked and fanned themselves on summer nights.

Indoors on cool evenings, the large rooms were lighted by candles in wall sconces. When there was company in drawing and dining rooms, a house slave lowered beautiful French chandeliers and lighted scores of candles. Their light glinted on imported mahogany, walnut, and fruit-wood furniture, and on ornately framed mirrors. Underfoot were Persian rugs. Here the plantation mistress and her daughters entertained the guests with the music of Mozart and Corelli, played on a spinet or harpsichord. Perhaps they sang French folk songs or one of the new Stephen Foster melodies that were all the rage, like "Oh, Susanna!" or "My Old Kentucky

Home." On such an evening each lady looked like a fashion plate, in satin hoopskirt, deeply cut neckline, and hair curled and piled high in the favored style of Napoleon's court. The young gentleman turning the music wore a velvet lounge jacket, ruffled shirt, and flowing black tie.

By contrast, in a New England farmhouse the kitchen, not the drawing room, was the heart of the home. Here was where the family, including farm hands and hired girl, gathered close to the fire to eat their meals and read the Bible, to bathe on a Saturday night, to knit and gossip with a neighbor, or to pull molasses taffy. Front parlors were left unwarmed and cheerless. Heavy curtains were drawn to keep the sun from fading the red carpet, except when the minister or great-aunt Hannah came for a visit. Then the good wife might light two tallow or bayberry candles of her own dipping and set them in her prize pewter holders.

Plantation kitchens were separated from the rest of the house by a covered runway. Except for their mistress, who supervised them daily and who unlocked the safe where the family silver, imported tea, sugar lumps, brandy, and spices were kept, only the cooking slaves stayed in the

Set amidst pine woods, a Southern distillery makes turpentine out of resin from the pines.

kitchen. Here heat from the enormous open fireplace, where food was broiled, roasted, and baked must have been unbearable for months of each year. There was little danger that, in such a climate, the food would cool too noticeably while being carried the long walkway from fire to the master's plate.

Some of the differences were economic, of course. The New England farmer's great-grandfather had had to clear his bleak acres not only of trees, roots, and vines, but also of stones that seemed to "bile" up out of the earth from planting time to planting time. There was no end to them. When harvested, these fields produced only enough food for the farmer's own family, seldom cash for their owner's pocket, or money to be spent on luxuries.

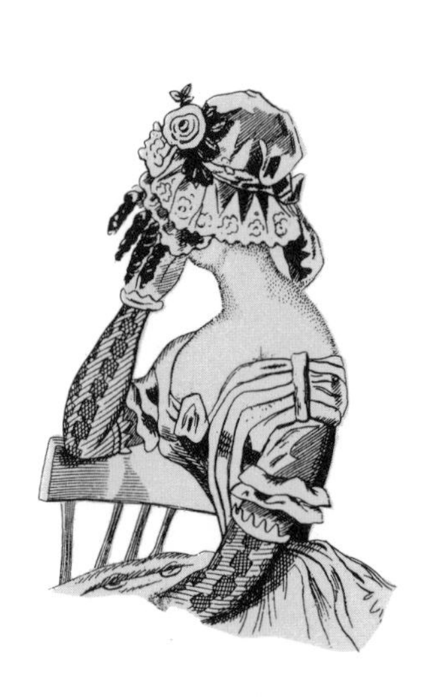

Crops raised on the plantation depended on the location. The plantation owner's great-grandfather had staked his claim or received it from the English King for large holdings of fertile black tidewater acres on Carolina, Virginia, or Georgia shores. Here the native American tobacco, to which Indians had introduced him, grew luxuriantly. European markets clamored to buy all he could cultivate of this New World product. Here, too, cotton from the West Indies became King of Crops, once northern spinning wheels began to whir. In South Carolina there were vast marshes just right for growing rice. And in Louisiana there was sugar cane, for which both Old and New World had developed a taste.

Godey's Lady's Book displayed these fashions in the fall of 1842.

On his trip through America in 1842, the celebrated English novelist, Charles Dickens, described a plantation home in these words:

> *The planter's house was an airy, rustic dwelling . . . The day was warm, but, the blinds all being closed, and the windows and doors set wide open, a shady coolness rustled through the rooms, which was exquisitely refreshing after the glare and heat without. Before the windows was an open piazza, where, in what they call the hot weather . . . they sling hammocks, and drink and doze luxuriously . . . I can report that . . . the mounds of ices and bowls of mint julep and sherry cobbler they make in these latitudes are refreshments never to be thought of afterwards, in summer, by those who would preserve contented minds.*

The "ices" mentioned by Dickens were chilled by chips of natural ice, great blocks of which had been cut from northern lakes in winter and shipped to southern ports, where they were stored in ice houses. What luxury—ice in the midst of a blazing southern summer!

Spoonbread and Sillabub

Plantation food, too, was delectable. Recipes handed down from mother to daughter were prized in every family. There was black walnut cake,

Not only did a lady ride side-saddle in the 1850's, but her habit was long and flowing.

layers high, hot spoonbread swimming in butter to eat with fried lake or brook trout, and shivering blancmange flavored with the rare extract of the vanilla bean. Many a plantation visitor later remembered being awakened at dawn by the dull, rhythmic "thud, thud" of a Negress beating unraised biscuit with a wooden paddle, for the master to eat with his breakfast ham. At Thanksgiving and Christmas there were smoked turkey stuffed with oyster dressing and ham boiled in apple cider. There was thick eggnog made with a dozen eggs and a quart of cream, wry-yet-sweet persimmon pudding, sillabub, and, served with fruit cake, an ambrosia of freshly grated coconut and fresh orange segments.

Food on even an ordinary day seemed worth remembering to Frederick Law Olmsted, a Northerner who kept a journal of his trip through the Southern states in mid-century. Even for breakfast, the variety of foods was astounding:

> *A stout woman acted as head waitress, employing two handsome little mulatto boys as her aids in communicating with the kitchen, from which relays of hot cornbread, of an excellence quite new to me, were brought at frequent intervals . . . There was but one vegetable served—sweet potatoes, roasted in ashes . . . but there were four preparations of swine's flesh,*

beside fried fowls, fried eggs, cold roast turkey, and opossum, cooked I know not how, but it somehow resembled baked suckling-pig.

Southern plantation life sounds like a replica of the centuries-old life of the French and English gentry: gracious, charming—and idle. This impression was partly calculated. It was part of the picture for the Southern planter to look relaxed and leisurely, for his lady to seem to be a fragile doll whose dainty hands never knew work of any kind. However, both master and mistress were, if conscientious, disciplined and busy people.

The planter spent endless hours at his desk arranging for the care of mansion, garden and field, barns, stables, cabins, and all their occupants, both animal and human. He had to arrange for the sale of his rice, tobacco, or cotton crop downriver or at the nearest port. He spent hours of each day riding from one end of the plantation to the other, to be sure that all went well with his people, equipment, and property. There was usually an overseer who took hourly responsibility for the field work. A large holding was like a small kingdom, in which the ruler made laws and saw that they were obeyed. He must also see personally to the welfare of his people.

Plantation Childhood

Babies were coddled and loved by two mothers—their own and a gentle Negro mammy. Little boys and girls played at indoor games under the eyes of a colored nursemaid. From their dark playmates the white children caught the soft, honeyed overtones that would color their voices for the rest of their lives. But almost from infancy both black and white child were aware of the gulf between them. It was the Negro who dug the worms for the day of fishing on the garden pond and who baited the hook for his young master, even at age eight or ten. When it was time to begin lessons, master's children and slave children were separated. It was against the law to teach one's slaves to read or write, for fear these skills might make them discontented with their lot in life. Now and then a generous-spirited mistress taught the brightest of the slave youngsters their letters, at her knee with her own children.

After ginning, the cotton was pressed, baled and carted to wharves on the Mississippi River.

Soon white brothers and sisters were also separated during school hours. The "young masters" were put under the care of a tutor who lived at the plantation house and taught the boys Latin and Greek, philosophy, logic, mathematics and French. The tutor was often a bright young man just graduated from Yale or the University of Virginia. In the afternoons these older boys practised riding and shooting—the gentlemanly sports. Sometimes at dawn they rode to hounds in the English tradition of the fox hunt.

Meanwhile the daughter of the home had begun the complicated business of learning to be a Southern lady. She must read well enough to understand her Bible and prayerbook, and to enjoy the stilted novels

thought fit for a young girl. Her brother's tutor gave her singing lessons, sometimes "French conversation." Her mother or maiden aunt taught her the intricate feather and crewel embroidery for decorating bed hangings and curtains, and delicate hairpin braid for baby clothes and her own petticoats. She learned to dance enchantingly, to curtsey modestly, and to flourish a carved ivory fan at a young gentleman.

The Slave Business

The whole plantation way of life was built upon the Negro slave. By the work of his hands and the sweat of his brow the great plantations were cultivated, planted, and harvested. Though slavery was outlawed early in the century, for many years thereafter hosts of native Africans were smuggled into Southern ports by Yankee ships engaged in the vicious three-way molasses, rum, and slave traffic. Thus it was not only Southern plantation owners who profited by the slave system but many a Yankee trader.

The slaves were chained and tied like animals in the dark holds of clipper ships for the duration of the long voyage from their African home. Once in the New World, they were sold—like animals—on an auction block in Charleston, New Orleans, Key West, and even Washington, D. C. A physically strong young man was sold as a "prime field hand" in 1825 for $500; on the eve of the Civil War the same young man was sold for $1800. A lesser price pas paid by another owner, whose home might be three states distant, for the slave's young sister who, though frail, might still be taught to become a good nursemaid or kitchen girl. To separate African families from each other and from members of their own tribe was considered insurance against a possible slave rebellion.

A scrub woman.

Some slave owners disapproved of a system that depended upon the slavery of the dark-skinned man and woman. These men had inherited their slaves, along with their great houses, their mother's silver tea service, and their father's library of rare Morocco-bound books. What could they do with this legacy of human beings except deal as justly as possible with them? Mary Todd Lincoln's own father in Lexington, Kentucky, was one of these. He had inherited a few house slaves and hardly knew what to do with them. A few such men freed their slaves. But where could such free Negroes find a job and a way of life in which they might be treated like other free men whose skins were white? In many Northern cities a Negro was feared and hated by a new emigrant to America as a possible threat to his own job as factory worker or laborer.

There was one who shared the master's duties and responsibility for the people of the plantation community. This was his wife. Under her delicate, ladylike exterior there often lay many practical skills, kindness and wisdom. Not all accounts, however, show the plantation mistress as sweetly selfless. Harriet Martineau, an English gentlewoman, wrote about her visit to a plantation in 1838:

You sit down to the piano or to read, and one slave or another enters every half hour to ask what is o'clock. Your hostess comes in at length, and you sit down to work with her; she gratifies your curiosity about "her people," telling you how soon they burn out their shoes at the toes, and wear out their winter woolens, and tear out their summer cottons; and how impossible it is to get black women to learn to cut out clothes without waste; and how she never inquires when and where the whipping is done, as it is the overseer's business, and not hers.

In the Slave Quarters

There were, of course, as many kinds of Negro slaves as there were other people. Some were strong of body and will, and some were weak. Some were proud sons and grandsons of African kings, and some were untrustworthy. Some were deeply religious; others lived in fear of strange voodoo magic and "conjuring," dimly remembered. On the plantation all these

The vast marshes of South Carolina were ideal for growing rice.

Life in "the quarters" was not all misery; sometimes the slaves found release in music and dancing.

were divided into house and field slaves and those who could be taught skills like blacksmithing, carpentry, or care of the horses. The brightest and best-tempered were the house servants.

Slave cabins or "the Quarters" were grouped like a village of log cabins, not too far behind the "great house." Each black family had its own cabin. There was a bare, swept yard where the children could roll and play. Behind it there was a little garden patch for growing turnip and collard greens to boil with white meat or fat back. Maybe there was room for a few watermelons. The master gave out cornmeal, pork, hominy grits, bacon, a little molasses, and salt each week on Ration Day. Frederick Law Olmsted, the Yankee who visited many plantations during his trip south, described a day in a field slave's life:

> *After breakfast has been eaten early in the cabins, at sunrise or a little before in winter . . . they go to the field. At noon dinner is brought to them, and, unless the work presses, they are allowed two hours' rest. Very punctually at sunset they stop work and are at liberty . . . Thus they work in the field about eleven hours a day . . . returning to the cabins . . . They then make a fire—a big blazing fire . . . for the supply of fuel is unlimited—and cook their own supper, which will be a bit*

of bacon fried, often with eggs, cornbread baked in the spider after the bacon, to absorb the fat, and perhaps some sweet potatoes roasted in the ashes. Immediately after supper they go to sleep, often lying on the floor or a bench in preference to a bed.

Such was a sample working day. There were also holidays. Almost any event could furnish an excuse for a celebration, such as Hog-Killin' Day, with dancing to follow, or Corn Huskin' Time, when slaves from a neighboring plantation were invited to enter the contest. The human heart, though oppressed, finds ways to express its light moods as well as its sad ones. At all times the Quarter was likely to be a noisy place, with scolding, fighting, gossip, merrymaking, and song.

America owes some of its most poignant native music to the Negro slaves. When the work of cotton-picking or stevedoring became too hard to bear, some black man with a rich and resonant voice knew how to make it seem lighter by starting a song. Some of these grew out of a spirit of fun, like "The Old Ark Was a Moverin'" or "Sit Down, Sinner. I Cain't Sit Down." Some were slow and deeply sorrowful, like "Nobody Knows the Trouble I've Seen." Many of these, such as "Swing Low, Sweet Chariot," expressed the deeply religious nature of these people. Theirs was a primitive faith, simple and childlike, but their spirituals have inspired multitudes of people the world around.

The slaves also gave us some of our best-loved folk tales. Retired from field or housework, there was always some snowy-haired old "Uncle Remus" who was an endless source of stories that he claimed to remember from his own parents or grandparents. Many were animal tales, dealing with "Brer Rabbit" and "Mister Fox," who showed very human weaknesses and cleverness. Almost always there was a moral, though so sugarcoated that no child could possibly object to swallowing it whole. Writers with white skins, like Joel Chandler Harris, have set down many of these tales for generations of children to read.

All told, the life of both white man and black, master and slave, of the Southern plantation was a mixture of kindness and injustice, pleasure and pain. It was a riddle that even a Civil War could not solve. Some of its problems are still unsolved, one hundred years later.

From River Boat to Iron Horse

3

It was one thing to stay comfortably at home in a trim cottage or snug farmhouse, but suppose you wished to visit grandparents two hundred miles away, or had a hundred bales of cotton to sell in a distant market. How did people travel across the land and transport goods a century and a half ago? The easiest road was the natural one—the river that flowed closest to your door and nearest to your destination. For rivers had forced their way through the wilderness long before man. True, they often followed meandering courses, and there were rapids and waterfalls that made overland portage necessary, but there was no mud and no dust. And travel through untamed country by water meant less danger of ambush from unfriendly Indians. So the rivers of America became its first highways.

The greatest of these, the Mississippi, was navigable for more than two thousand miles, and it also had a vast network of tributaries. Some of these, such as the Tennessee, the Ohio, and the Missouri, were important rivers in their own right. How much time and labor it would have taken to chop even the crudest of roads through all these miles of forest. Small wonder that, from the moment of its discovery, the Mississippi was used as a north-south highway for carrying people, timber, coal, cotton, and household goods.

Barge, Keelboat and Flatboat

The earliest river travel was by canoe, but by 1800, barges, keelboats, and flatboats were also in use. All of these, however, were kinds of rafts, many without built-up sides or cabins. Some were enormous—almost a square acre of flat pine boards, with wigwams on them for shelter in bad weather. As a boy in Hannibal, Missouri, Mark Twain would swim out to such rafts and hitch rides downriver for the fun of it. Later, he made Tom Sawyer and Huck Finn do this in his books.

Some boats were fitted with sails, but more often they simply drifted south, and then were laboriously poled back north against the strong Mississippi currents. Sometimes large-bladed oars called "sweeps" were used for rowing. A journey downriver and back took as long as nine

With a wary eye for snags and for the wash of passing steamboats, the keelsman maneuvered his giant sweep.

Travel on some Mississippi steamboats was scarcely a hardship.

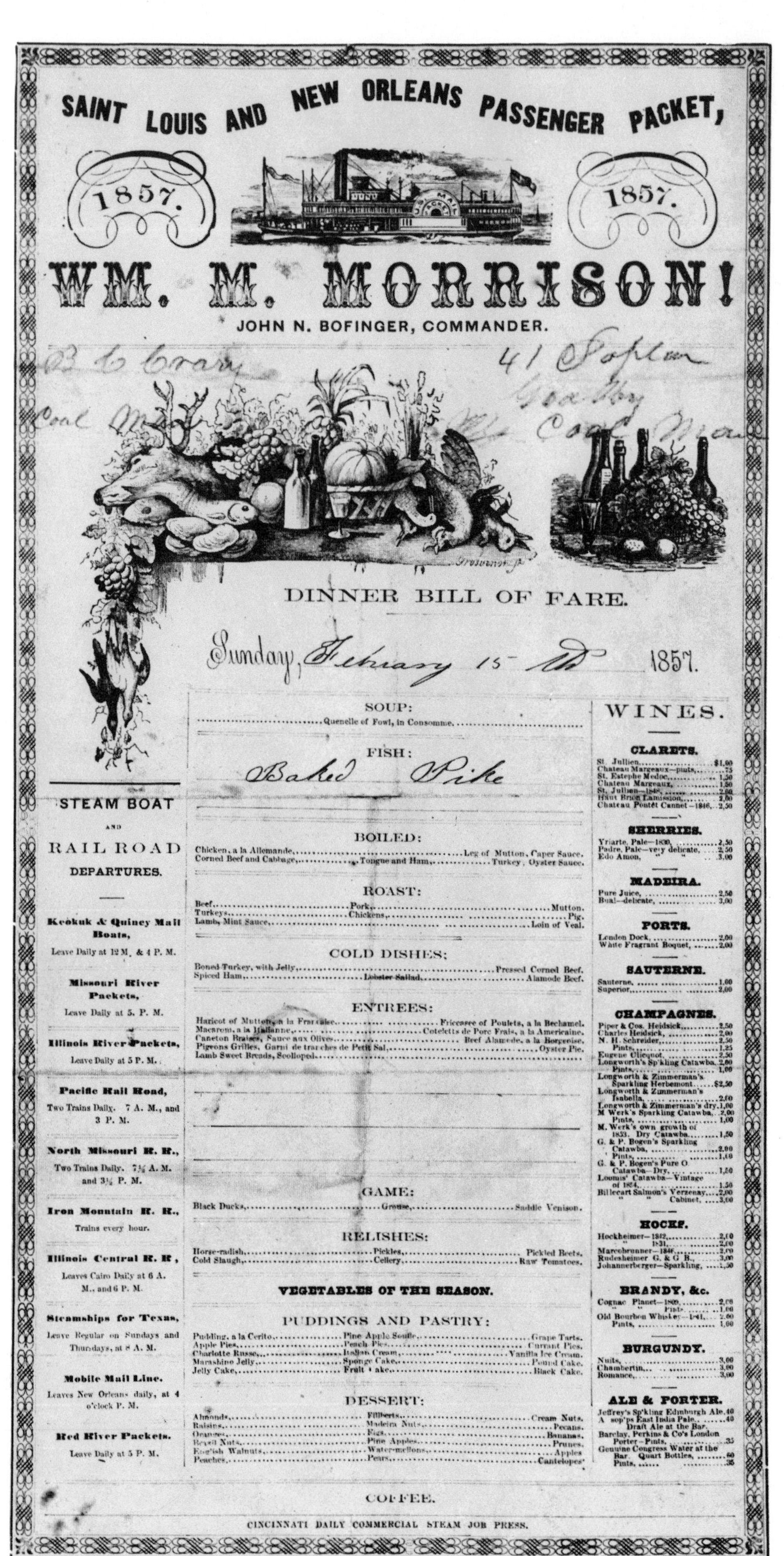

SAINT LOUIS AND NEW ORLEANS PASSENGER PACKET,

1857. 1857.

WM. M. MORRISON!

JOHN N. BOFINGER, COMMANDER.

DINNER BILL OF FARE.

Sunday, February 15th 1857.

SOUP:

Quenelle of Fowl, in Consomme.

FISH:

Baked Pike

BOILED:

Chicken, a la Allemande, ... Leg of Mutton, Caper Sauce.
Corned Beef and Cabbage, ... Tongue and Ham, ... Turkey, Oyster Sauce.

ROAST:

Beef, ... Pork, ... Mutton.
Turkeys, ... Chickens, ... Pig.
Lamb, Mint Sauce, ... Loin of Veal.

COLD DISHES:

Boned Turkey, with Jelly, ... Pressed Corned Beef.
Spiced Ham, ... Lobster Sallad, ... Alamode Beef.

ENTREES:

Haricot of Mutton, a la Francaise ... Fricassee of Poulets, a la Bechamel.
Macaroni, a la Italianne, ... Cotelettes de Porc Frais, a la Americaine.
Caneton Braises, Sauce aux Olives ... Beef Alamode, a la Borgeoise.
Pigeons Grilles, Garni de tranches de Petit Sal, ... Oyster Pie.
Lamb Sweet Breads, Scolloped ...

GAME:

Black Ducks, ... Grouse, ... Saddle Venison.

RELISHES:

Horse-radish, ... Pickles, ... Pickled Beets.
Cold Slaugh, ... Cellery, ... Raw Tomatoes.

VEGETABLES OF THE SEASON.

PUDDINGS AND PASTRY:

Pudding, a la Cerito, ... Pine Apple Soufle, ... Grape Tarts.
Apple Pies, ... Peach Pies, ... Currant Pies.
Charlotte Russe, ... Italian Cream, ... Vanilla Ice Cream.
Marashino Jelly, ... Sponge Cake, ... Pound Cake.
Jelly Cake, ... Fruit Cake, ... Black Cake.

DESSERT:

Almonds, ... Filberts, ... Cream Nuts.
Raisins, ... Madeira Nuts, ... Pecans.
Oranges, ... Figs, ... Bananas.
Brazil Nuts, ... Pine Apples, ... Prunes.
English Walnuts, ... Water-mellons, ... Apples
Peaches, ... Pears, ... Cantelopes.

COFFEE.

STEAM BOAT AND RAIL ROAD DEPARTURES.

Keokuk & Quincy Mail Boats,
Leave Daily at 12 M. & 4 P. M.

Missouri River Packets,
Leave Daily at 5. P. M.

Illinois River Packets,
Leave Daily at 5 P. M.

Pacific Rail Road,
Two Trains Daily. 7 A. M., and 3 P. M.

North Missouri R. R.,
Two Trains Daily. 7½ A. M. and 3½ P. M.

Iron Mountain R. R.,
Trains every hour.

Illinois Central R. R.,
Leaves Cairo Daily at 6 A. M., and 6 P. M.

Steamships for Texas,
Leave Regular on Sundays and Thursdays, at 8 A. M.

Mobile Mail Line.
Leaves New Orleans daily, at 4 o'clock P. M.

Red River Packets.
Leave Daily at 5 P. M.

WINES.

CLARETS.

St. Jullien, ... $1,00
Chateau Margeaux—pints, ... 75
St. Estephe Medoc, ... 1,50
Chateau Margeaux, ... 1,50
St. Jullien—1848, ... 2,00
Haut Brion Lamission, ... 2,00
Chateau Poutet Cannet—1846, ... 2,50

SHERRIES.

Yriarte, Pale—1830, ... 2,50
Padre, Pale—very delicate, ... 2,50
Edo Amon, " " ... 3,00

MADEIRA.

Pure Juice, ... 2,50
Bual—delicate, ... 3,00

PORTS.

London Dock, ... 2,00
White Fragrant Boquet, ... 2,00

SAUTERNE.

Sauterne, ... 1,00
Superior, ... 2,00

CHAMPAGNES.

Piper & Cos. Heidsick, ... 2,50
Charles Heidsick, ... 2,00
N. H. Schreider, ... 2,50
Pints, ... 1,25
Eugene Clicquot, ... 2,50
Longworth's Sp'kling Catawba, ... 2,00
Pints, ... 1,00
Longworth & Zimmerman's Sparkling Herbemont ... $2,50
Longworth & Zimmerman's Isabella, ... 2,00
Longworth & Zimmerman's dry ... 1,00
M Werk's Sparkling Catawba, ... 2,00
Pints, ... 1,00
M. Werk's own growth of 1853. Dry Catawba ... 1,50
G. & P. Bogen's Sparkling Catawba, ... 2,00
Pints, ... 1,10
G. & P. Bogen's Pure O. Catawba—Dry, ... 1,50
Loomis' Catawba—Vintage of 1854, ... 1,50
Billecart Salmon's Verzenay, ... 2,00
" " Cabinet, ... 3,00

HOCKS.

Hockheimer—1842, ... 2,10
" 1831, ... 2,00
Marcobrunner—1846, ... 2,00
Rudesheimer G. & G B., ... 3,00
Johannerberger—Sparkling, ... 2,50

BRANDY, &c.

Cognac Planet—1809, ... 2,00
" " Pints ... 1,00
Old Bourbon Whiskey—1841, ... 2,00
Pints, ... 1,00

BURGUNDY.

Nuits, ... 3,00
Chambertin, ... 3,00
Romance, ... 3,00

ALE & PORTER.

Jeffrey's Sp'kling Edinburgh Ale .40
Allsop's East India Pale, ... 40
Draft Ale at the Bar.
Barclay, Perkins & Co's London Porter—Pints, ... 35
Genuine Congress Water at the Bar. Quart Bottles, ... 60
Pints, ... 35

CINCINNATI DAILY COMMERCIAL STEAM JOB PRESS.

The dining room of the steamboat "Great Republic" in 1870.

months. The keelsmen (about two dozen for a large boat) were strong, hardy men—rough of manner, dress and tongue. At the end of each trip, in St. Louis or New Orleans, they squandered their hard-earned pay.

Young Abe Lincoln knew what it was like to take a cargo of farm produce a thousand miles down the Mississippi River on a flatboat, one that he himself had built. Like other keelsmen, he had held his breath when a strong current threatened to sweep the boat out of control of his long oars. He knew, too, what it was like to be caught on a snag of roots or to flounder in the wake of a great steamboat.

"S-t-e-a-mboat A-comin'!"

The keelboat was too slow to suit an inventor from New York state named Robert Fulton. For years he had been experimenting with a boat which would, he hoped, propel itself by steam. As one after another of his models failed, he grew used to being the laughingstock of his neighbors. One day in 1807, he tried out his newest boat, the *Clermont,* on the Hudson River. As usual, a few doubters had gathered on the banks to watch and to jeer,

The Albany Basin of the Erie Canal shows how popular this new waterway had become by the 1850's.

when suddenly the "steamboat" began furiously churning water. Then, wonder of wonders, with its twin smokestacks puffing clouds of smoke and steam, the boat slipped from its moorings and began chugging upstream—against the current, and without manpower! As the watchers looked on in awe, she steamed out of sight, never pausing until she reached Albany—150 miles in thirty-two hours! "Fulton's Folly," as people called the little boat, soon revolutionized traffic on river, lake, and ocean the world around. In America the steamboat was to bring excitement, color, and a thousand new products and ideas to remote river towns just carved from the wilderness.

The popularity of the keelboat did not die out immediately, however, and passengers and cargoes continued to drift downriver on flatboats in the old way. But now those going up-river steamed back on the new "swimming volcanoes." Abraham Lincoln did just this in 1829. After a three-month journey down the Mississippi on a flatboat with his friend, Allen Gentry, the two young men returned on an elegant "river queen."

Steamboats were more and more in demand. Indeed, the fifty years after 1820 are often called the "Steamboat Era." Great fortunes were made by the owners of such vessels; other fortunes were made by the plantation owners who used the boats to send cotton and sugar to market in New Orleans, Natchez, Memphis, and St. Louis. Instead of white keelsmen, the new boats had Negro roustabouts who hustled the great bales and boxes in and out of the holds at every landing.

With the addition of a second deck and the huge side paddlewheels, the great boats became "floating palaces," their interiors patterned after fashionable hotel lobbies. There were Persian rugs, crystal chandeliers, curlicued woodwork, murals of birds and flowers, mirrored bars, barber shops, and orchestras. Outside, the boats were painted white, or brilliant reds and blues. At the height of their fame, Mississippi steamboats were often called "Floating Wedding Cakes."

And what dinners were served! Boat owners vied with each other to employ famous chefs. Menus contained as many as seven soups, scores of main dishes, and fifteen different desserts. And all this luxury was found in a country that only recently had belonged to Indian bear, and wildcat! In his *Life on the Mississippi,* Mark Twain wrote of the excitement that swept sleepy river towns when "S-t-e-a-mboat a-comin'!" sounded through the streets:

> *The town drunkard stirs, the clerks wake up, a furious clatter of drays follows, every house and store pours out a human contribution, and all in a twinkling the dead town is alive and moving. Drays, carts, men, boys, all go hurrying from many quarters to a common center, the wharf. Assembled there, the people fasten their eyes upon the coming boat as upon a wonder they are seeing for the first time . . . the pent steam is screaming through the gauge cocks; the captain lifts his hand, a bell rings, the wheels stop . . . Then such a scramble as there*

After the canalboat has moved into place between the two locks, water will be let in or out depending on the direction in which the boat is going.

Coaches as well as cattle stopped to pay fees at tollhouses.

is to get aboard, and to get ashore, and to take in freight and to discharge freight, all at one and the same time; and such a yelling and cursing as the mates facilitate it all with. Ten minutes later the steamer is under way again, and the town drunkard asleep by the skids once more.

Those were the days when small boys up and down the Mississippi wanted more than anything else to be river pilots. Such pilots maneuvered their vessels "by guess and by gum"—a mixture of intuition, memory and hard-earned skill. For "Ole Man River" was not to be fully trusted. There were treacherous shoals and sandbanks, constantly shifting. There were snags, fogs, drifting logs, and sudden squalls. There were other dangers—among them human folly. For one thing, gamblers flourished on the steamboats, practicing their trickery while dressed like gentlemen in the flowered waistcoat, swallowtail fashion of the day. Worse than these, it became a real but sometimes disastrous sport to try to set records for speed. Passengers and crew alike were thrilled when two riverboat captains challenged each other to a race upriver. The dangers of a burst boiler or fire were forgotten and the winner enjoyed the title of "King of the River."

Low Bridges and Big Ditches

America was fortunate not only in her natural highways, the rivers, but also in her lakes. Soon the problem was how to join rivers and lakes in a continuous passage to make the way West easier for the thousands of Easterners attacked by "Ohio Fever." The overland way was grueling, and no river flowed from East to West, cutting across the barrier of the Allegheny Mountains.

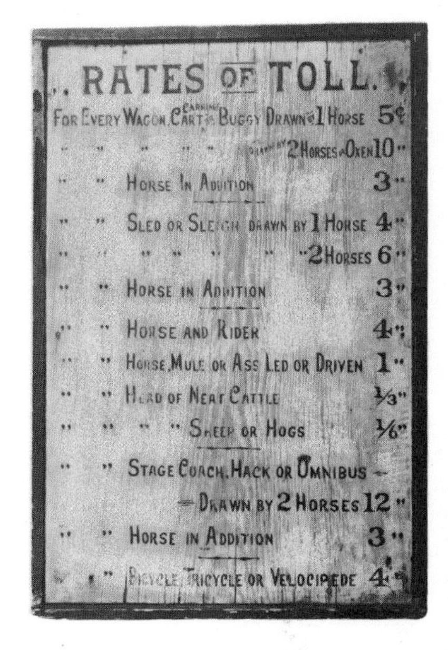

A toll chart

Early in the nation's history, far-sighted men had thought of digging canals to speed the westward trek. Many short canals were dug. The most famous and longest, the Erie Canal, was completed in 1825 and ran from the town of Buffalo on Lake Erie to Albany—across New York State. Barges, flatboats, and packets were poled through this canal and its many locks; some, however, were pulled by mules along a towpath for 363 miles between western New York and the Hudson River. Cargoes and passengers could then float down to New York City, and from there go around the world by clipper ship.

Thomas Woodcock, a New York engraver who made the trip by canal from Schenectady to Buffalo, wrote that the captain was "a genteel man," and that "passengers ate their meals with the best *silver* plate." His ticket for the distance, eighty miles, cost three dollars, and included a dinner of four or five kinds of meat and fowl, hot breads aplenty, enormous bowls of vegetables, seven or eight kinds of cake and pie. No wonder captains had to set a watch at every bridge to keep spongers from jumping aboard for a "free" meal, then slipping away quietly at the next bridge without paying a penny's fare.

Mr. Woodcock made special note in his journal of the lowness of bridges crossing the canal. Before passing under one, the helmsman called out "bridge," "*very* low bridge," or "the *lowest* in the canal." Then it was up to every passenger to bend low or to lie flat on deck.

As for travel on the Great Lakes, in 1835 Miss Ellen Bigelow made a trip across Lake Erie from Buffalo to Chicago. Because she knew that a steamboat might blow up, she chose an old-fashioned sailing vessel. Unfortunately, the one she chose was so loaded with freight that there was no room for passengers on the deck. This meant a disagreeable passage, with thirty men, women, and children crowded day and night into a small cabin. Though it was May, the sailing boat had to wait at the wharf for several days until the last of the winter ice melted. It sailed in a storm so severe that Miss Bigelow became "lakesick." Later, the boat stuck on a shoal and there was even danger of its sinking. Finally it went aground outside Detroit harbor.

The Hazards of Land Travel

What if no river or canal lapped the shore of your home town or of your destination, or if you needed to journey during winter, when waterways had a habit of freezing over? In short, what about land travel?

The sad truth is that there were too few roads of any kind. The nation's proudest cities along the Eastern seaboard were joined, if at all, by the crudest roads. Old Indian trails just wide enough for a rider on horseback were more common.

Abigail Adams, wife of the newly elected President of the United States, wrote in 1800 of her difficulties in going from Baltimore to Washington to join her husband in the brand-new White House. After only eight or nine miles on "the Frederick Road" (one of the few "good" roads in the nation), she and her companions became lost in a trackless wilderness for two hours. Finally a Negro was hired to guide the party through a forest that went to the very edge of the capital.

Horseback was still the surest way to travel. But not everyone was an accomplished rider. Fewer still cared to walk—or, as the saying went, to "ride shanks' mare"—for long distances. Americans yearned for the ancient turnpikes of Europe, down which it was usually possible to travel by stagecoach, private carriage, oxcart, or horsedrawn wagon. But how were wide roads to be hacked out of dense forests even in the "civilized" Eastern states?

In 1802, Congress chose an ancient buffalo trace to turn into the first National Road. Known as "Uncle Sam's Pike" it took fifteen long years to build and was only a scant ninety miles when finished. At first it ran from Cumberland in Maryland, the head of navigation on the Potomac River, to Wheeling, West Virginia. Not until 1852 was it extended as far west as Vandalia, Illinois. No one today would call it a road at all. Never surfaced with more than a layer of gravel, it was constantly in a state of deep mud, choking dust, or frozen ruts. A Methodist bishop who had journeyed

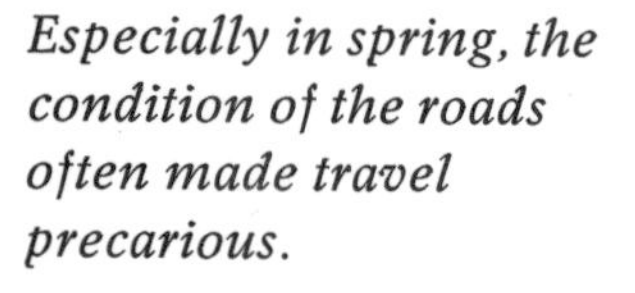

Especially in spring, the condition of the roads often made travel precarious.

Hostlers waste no time in changing horses so that the mail coach may continue on its way.

on "Uncle Sam's Pike" wrote that it was "intolerable, shocking, wretched, and devilish." Horses died trying to pull their wagons out of the mire. Bridges were washed away by violent mountain storms. Despite all this, the Cumberland Road became the popular way to the new West, alive with brightly painted stagecoaches, covered wagons and their families, and whole flocks of livestock being driven on foot.

Mrs. Frances Trollope, an Englishwoman who traveled in America in 1830, wrote of a stagecoach journey on the Cumberland Road. She described being tossed about with the other passengers "like a few potatoes in a wheelbarrow." She was kept too busy protecting herself from bruises and possible dislocation even to glance out of the window at the beautiful mountain country. Only when the coach stopped could she admire the view. Mrs. Trollope found many things to complain about in brash, raw America, but she wrote glowingly of the beauty of the virgin hemlocks, rushing streams, azaleas, rhododendron, "shumac," and laurel.

When night came, however, she had this complaint of her treatment at a mountain inn:

> *Arrived at our inn, a forlorn parlour, filled with . . . fumes of tobacco . . . received us; and chilled, as we began to feel ourselves with the mountain air, we preferred going to our cold bedrooms rather than sup in such an atmosphere. We found linen on the beds which they assured us had only been in use* a few nights . . .
>
> . . . *It was . . . with great difficulty that we procured a fire in*

Riders of the Pony Express carried news from coast to coast in less than ten days.

our bedrooms from the surly-looking young lady *who condescended to officiate as chamber-maid, and with much more that we extorted clean linen for our beds; that done, we patiently crept into them supperless, while she made her exit muttering about the difficulty of "fixing English folks."*

Next morning, however, things looked brighter. Mrs. Trollope wrote of the delicious mountain food the stagecoach passengers were served at breakfast: wild turkey and mountain venison, vegetables that were "extremely fine," and wild strawberries! Sad to report, not all stagecoach stops were so pleasant. For years there were few inns—only stray farmhouses at irregular intervals on the turnpike. These sometimes rented a pile of straw and a blanket in a corner near the hearth to a few weary travelers. And the food offered was more often cornmeal mush than venison.

One tall tale tells of a half-mile stretch on a "highway" that was in such unexpectedly good condition that a delighted traveler drove his buggy back and forth all day long "to get the good out of it." Another describes a rider who, after nearly drowning with his horse in a boggy place, put up this sign:

This place is not crossible,
Not even horsible.

A stagecoach passenger on a new log, or corduroy, road in South Carolina left a swamp story: he complained to the driver that wind, whistling through holes in the floor, made his feet intolerably cold. Soon, however, he discovered the reason for the holes; when at one place the road and the coach were flooded by swamp water, the passengers had to ride on the roof. When they came to a dry place again, the water in the coach ran out freely through the holes!

A fast coach traveling a good road could make 100 to 125 miles in a twenty-four hour day, stopping only at intervals for a change of horses and a new driver. Poor, bone-weary passengers who rode all day and night without relief! But the view from the coach window seldom lacked interest, for the road swarmed with traffic. Fortesque Cuming, a New Yorker who journeyed into the Ohio country to inspect land he had just bought, wrote:

> *Apropos of travelling there are Packers with from one to twenty horses, selling or trucking their wares through the country;—Countrymen, sometimes alone, sometimes in large companies, carrying salt . . . for the curing of their beef, pork, venison, etc.;—Families, removing farther back into the country, some with cows, oxen, horses, sheep, and hogs, and all their farming implements and domestick utensils, and some without . . . The residue . . . are country merchants, judges and lawyers attending the courts, members of the legislature, and the better class of settlers.*

What hacking and hewing and stump-pulling it took to chop those first rough roads through the wilderness. And what jostling, jerking, and straining it took to travel them! But once built, they were so important

In 1859 the New York Central introduced something new—sleeping cars!

that it is easy to see why the years from 1790 to 1820 were called the Turnpike Era.

Pony Express

Once the Pacific Coast was well settled after the Gold Rush of 1849, the problem was: How were news, goods, and of course people to be carried all those thousands of difficult miles?

In 1858, a New York business man established the Butterfield Express, a stagecoach system that ran from Missouri to California. At breakneck speed it transported passengers, parcels, and mails 2800 miles in twenty-five days of continuous travel. In addition to exhaustion from traveling for a solid month, there was constant danger of Indian ambush and highway robbery.

But almost a month from coast to coast was not fast enough, so a Mr. William Russell proposed the Pony Express. Everyone scoffed. It would surely take seventeen or eighteen days for the fastest rider to cross the country. Mr. Russell made a wager of $ 200,000 that his riders could make the trip in less than ten days. He won the bet. The first experimental Pony Express trip took nine days and seventeen hours. Soon the Pony Express was in operation. In mid-November 1860, one of its first messages sent the breadth of the continent was the news, "Lincoln's elected!" The newly invented telegraph and the Pony Express, working together, made it possible for San Francisco newspapers to print election news "ONLY SEVEN DAYS FROM THE EAST!"

The Pony Express lasted only a brief time, however, for the telegraph

took its place in 1862. But it had filled an important function in the westward expansion of America.

The Iron Horse

Meanwhile in Wales, in 1804, the first steam engine on wheels had propelled itself—to the wonder and consternation of onlookers. By 1811, this first locomotive, now moving on a track, had pulled ten tons of iron, plus five wagons carrying seventy men. Then, in the United States, in 1828, the Baltimore and Ohio Railroad began carrying people on a thirteen-mile strip of track.

But, at first, it was difficult to persuade the public that any engine could be stronger than a horse. A young inventor named Peter Cooper had by this time built a tiny steam locomotive which he called the "Tom Thumb" and he now offered to race his little engine against any horse in the land. A stagecoach company accepted the challenge. Bets were placed, most of them against the steam-puffing "teakettle-on-a-track." Sad to say, the train lost the race; but Peter Cooper had, of course, been right. Before many years had passed, the rumble of a train on its track was a familiar sound to thousands of Americans.

What courage was needed by those first railway passengers! First, there was the "fearful speed" of twenty and even thirty miles an hour; then, rails were apt to spread with heat or contract with cold; engine boilers, fired too hard, sometimes burst; cars caught fire from sparks; and couplers between carriages broke.

In 1831, the Mohawk and Hudson Railroad opened a new seventeen-

Excitement mounted as Peter Cooper's "Tom Thumb" overtook the horsecar in a race in 1830.

mile line from Albany to Schenectady, New York. The coaches were stagecoach bodies set on wheeled trucks. Coupled together with slack chains, the cars collided resoundingly whenever the train stopped. Hapless passengers were jerked "out from under their hats . . . or flying from the seats." Dry pitch was used for fuel, and as it burned, great clouds of black smoke loaded with flying sparks and live coals poured from the locomotive's stack. Many passengers on the memorable first ride brought umbrellas. But as soon as these were opened, the cloth was burned right off the frames. Some of the passengers themselves caught fire, so that they had to beat each other to put out the flames. By the end of the seventeen miles, their clothes were streaked, dingy, frizzled, and scorched.

Many families in wagons or buggies had gathered close to the tracks

Old-fashioned sleds pick up passengers from the new "Iron Horse."

to watch the dragon that breathed sparks. Both they and their horses were so terrified by the speed, smoke, sparks, clanging bell, and shrieking whistle, that horses bolted and buggies and wagons were overturned.

Soon, however, improved locomotives were built, and better rails were laid. Gangs of workmen, risking malaria, pushed the rail lines through swamps full of "solid miles of musquitoes." They felled the giant trees of virgin forest, rooted out stumps, and laid the metal-capped, oaken rails that were finally to tie the whole of America from Atlantic to Pacific. Newspaper editors wrote such editorials as this one:

> *Twenty miles an hour . . . why you wouldn't be able to keep an apprentice boy at work! Every Saturday evening, he must make*

Sad to relate, the railroads brought disaster as well as speedy transportation.

> *a trip to Ohio to spend Sunday with his sweetheart. Grave, plodding citizens will be flying about like comets. . . . It will encourage flightiness of intellect. Veracious people will turn into the most immeasurable liars. . . .*

Or they ranted like this:

> *It will upset the gravity of the nation . . . a pestilential, topsy-turvy, harum-scarum whirligig, the train. Give me the old solemn, straight-forward, regular canal—three miles an hour for express, with a yoke of oxen for heavy loads. I go for beasts of burden, it is more scriptural, and suits a moral and religious people better—none of your hop, skip, and jump whimsies for me!*

But there was something romantic about the train, something that made the blood tingle. Charles Dickens, author of *David Copperfield* and *Oliver Twist*, who made a train trip from Boston to Lowell, Massachusetts, in 1842, wrote:

> *. . . the train whirls headlong, dives through the woods again, emerges in the light, clatters over frail arches, rumbles upon the heavy ground, shoots beneath a wooden bridge which inter-*

cepts the light for a second like a wink, suddenly awakens all the slumbering echoes in the main street of a large town, and dashes on haphazard, pell-mell, neck-or-nothing, down the middle of the road. There— with . . . unaccustomed horses plunging and rearing, close to the very rails—there—on, on, on—tears the mad dragon of an engine with its train of cars; scattering in all directions a shower of burning sparks from its wood fire; screeching, hissing, yelling, panting; until at last the thirsty monster stops beneath a covered way to drink, the people cluster round, and you have time to breathe again.

Once established in the minds of the people as the marvel of the century, there was no stopping the expansion of the rail lines. By 1850 there was a railway between the Atlantic and Chicago; there were long lines laid north and south; and the suggestion had even been made that some day there ought to be a railroad all the way from Lake Erie to Oregon. And this at a time when there were only two states (Louisiana and Oregon) west of the Mississippi. But the idea caught fire. Only the Civil War held back the new American Dream: to extend the Dragon-That-Breathes-Sparks from the Atlantic to the Pacific Ocean.

Passengers packed their belongings in cardboard bandboxes. This gaily-colored box is decorated with a view of the Capitol at Washington.

"Pleasuring"

4

Our great-great-grandparents had no television or movies, no record players or outboard motors. They didn't need summer camps and they did not even have automobiles in which to take a Sunday drive. But let no one think that they had no pastimes. Were they here today, they might even feel a little sorry for us because we are missing many of their sources of entertainment.

Play—Country Style

Some of this "pleasuring," as they called it, was really work that they converted into fun by doing it in the company of other people. This is a secret the twentieth century has unfortunately forgotten. When a task is shared, it often does not seem like work. This was true of the quilting bee, the cider-making, the barn raising, the corn-shucking, and the sugaring-off party. All these centered around work that had to be done. The quilt with a "wedding ring" design needed stitching for the bride-to-be; the barn roof would have taken one man, even with sons, a week to raise without extra help; maple sap seems to take forever to reach the sugaring-off stage if you are waiting for it by yourself. So it happened that our nineteenth-century forebears invented parties with which to make work seem easier.

Folk traditions were sometimes built around these gay country events. At the husking bee the young man who found the rare "red ear" was allowed to kiss the girl of his choice. At the apple party, where the fruit was peeled, cored, and strung up to the rafters for drying, every girl tried to pare a whole apple in one single peel. Then she flung the paring over her left shoulder. If it fell to the floor still unbroken, the ribbon of apple skin was supposed to form the shape of her sweetheart's first initial.

Winter was the best time of year for country pleasuring, for there was less farm work then. Besides, it was far easier to travel by sleigh on the hard-packed snow than by wagon or even horseback during muddy or dusty seasons. In winter the young people of two villages could challenge each other to a toboggan race. Sleighs crowded with boys and girls would skim across the crisp snow to a neighboring village. There, the rival teams would race each other. Afterwards, at a party in the village hall, there would be hot spiced cider and doughnuts, and perhaps a square dance or two.

The guests watch the apple paring to see if it will form the shape of her sweetheart's initial.

Winter also meant easier hunting, with animal tracks traceable in the snow. It meant fishing through holes in the ice on a nearby pond—with tiny shacks, tents, or teepees of the Indian kind, even small fires set on the thick ice to lessen the possibility of frozen fingers and toes. There was also, in lake country, the excitement of races between ice sailboats equipped with both steel runners and sails. They required handy crews and a stiff winter wind. Currier and Ives, well-known engraver-artists of the time, left many pictures which make these wintertime country pleasures vivid for us today.

Indoors there was the ancient game of checkers enjoyed by countless men and boys in front of their home firesides or near the red-hot stove of the country store. Periodically there were town-wide or inter-village contests to determine the local champion.

Sugaring Off

The sugaring-off party was a favorite in the North. With the first sign of winter's softening, in February or March, family and friends piled into

At a cornhusking a boy could steal a kiss if he found a red ear, but if he turned up a black ear, his face was smudged with lampblack.

HOMER

sleighs. To the ringing of bells hung on the horses' harness, the sleighs were pulled across the crusty snow to the sugar camp. Here, with the first rising of the sap in his "sugar bush" or clump of hard maple, rock maple, or sugar maple trees, the owner had hung little wooden buckets beneath slashes cut in the trunks. Indians had taught the early settlers how to do this. In the Algonquin language, Red Men called maple sugar *sinzibuckwud,* meaning "drawn from wood."

A full-grown maple tree gives about two pailfuls of sap a day, which, when boiled down, yields a pound or so of sugar. For days before the sugaring-off party, boys emptied the buckets regularly, carried tubs of the sap on sleds to the "sugar house" and poured it into an enormous kettle. Here, on the evening of the party, women and girls stood guard over the bubbling sap, skimming off twigs and impurities, watching for the moment of "sugaring." If the syrup threatened to boil over, a piece of lard or butter the size of a nutmet was dropped into the hot sap. Now and then a spoonful of syrup was dropped onto a snowbank and, when cool enough, was rubbed between thumb and forefingers for testing—just as fudge is tested. When the sample turned "brittle as rosin," it was pronounced done. Then some of the hot syrup was poured into molds to harden as sugar. At a party, however, most was poured out on the snow to be pulled like taffy by sticky young people in pairs. And all took place on a clear, frosty night by the flickering light of the fire.

Holidays and Weddings

A step in making apple cider: the wheel crushed the apples against the wooden paddle.

Of course, holidays were made-to-order for celebrations. Thanksgiving was the most American one of all, and had been so ever since Governor Bradford had declared such a day for Massachusetts Bay Colony in 1621. But it was not until 1863 that Abraham Lincoln declared that a day of nation-wide Thanksgiving should be observed in November.

Edward Everett Hale has described a New England Thanksgiving of 1820 which might almost be the same one you and I celebrated last November. After telling of the special church service in the morning, he writes:

> *You began (eating) with your chicken pie and your roast turkey. You ate as much as you could, and you then ate what you could of mince pie, squash pie, Marlborough pie, cranberry tart, and plum pudding. Then you went to work on the fruits as you could . . . And when at last the last philopoena had been given between two of the children . . . all parties slid from their chairs, or rose up from them, as the length of their legs might be, and adjourned to the large parlor again.*
>
> *Before long we would be in the corner playing commerce, or old maid, or possibly "slap everlasting;" or the Game of Human Life . . .*

Children gather round as a spoonful of maple syrup is dropped on to a snowbank to harden it for eating.

The Marlborough pie, an old cookbook tells us, is a cross between a lemon pie and a custard. A philopoena is a nut with a double kernel that is shared by a couple; each promises to pay a forfeit if either fails to keep some pledge.

Hale also remembered vividly the Election Day of his early nineteenth-century boyhood. Like our Fair Day, it was held on the village green, with hucksters setting up booths and tents for selling such goodies as tamarinds (much like our tangerines), hot oysters, cold spruce beer (at two cents a full glass, one cent for a half-glass) and bright-colored candies. Mr. Hale's mother gave each of her own and each of the servants' children a "nine-

Stirring oratory before an election.

pence," or twelve cents, to spend. This they called their "'Lection Money."

The Fourth of July was another red-letter day. This was a time of speeches and of marching to a band made up of bugle, fife, and a patched-up drum. Sometimes a sham battle was fought by decrepit militiamen dressed in faded uniforms and carrying rusty muskets. Militia Day itself was held year after year in the early 1800's, with all able-bodied male citizens obliged to appear in uniform and be counted. Gradually this observance became a farce and was abandoned.

On holidays, a newfangled balloon was often exhibited as one of the wonders of the world. Billboards announcing that a man would risk his life by riding in the tiny basket dangling from a giant balloon were enough to entice hundreds of people from the surrounding country side to the town. Not all such exhibitions were entirely successful. The New York *Illustrated News* in 1860 recorded:

> *La Mountain, the balloonist, met with a serious accident on his recent voyage from Albany. He travelled thirty miles in twenty-nine minutes, and in attempting to land at East Lanesboro, Massachusetts, was caught in a tornado, and dashed against a stone wall, knocking him senseless, but breaking no bones.*

It is a hard to believe, but Christmas was not much observed by our nineteenth-century ancestors. No doubt this was partly because of the long-lasting Puritan influence. Those devout souls had scorned the frivolity of the Old English observance of the Christ Child's birthday. But plantation families of the Old South remembered the holly, the mistletoe, and the yule log of the Old Country. They enjoyed a Christmas feast of roast suckling pig with an apple in its mouth. They gave presents to each other and to their slaves. But not until the 1850's did the general American observance of Christmas begin to match that of Thanksgiving. Then children began looking forward to receiving the great treat of an orange or two, some candy, and a small toy on Christmas morning.

The Christmas tree came to America from Germany. Some think it was brought to our shores by Hessian soldiers who fought as mercenaries in the Revolution. The lovely idea of an evergreen tree—trimmed with colored scraps of ribbon and paper, gingerbread cookies in fancy shapes, strings of popcorn and cranberries, perhaps even a few small wax candles and a tinfoil star—spread fast among pleasure-loving Pennsylvania Germans and light-hearted Southerners. Finally, even sober New Englanders could resist its charm no longer.

Then there was St. Valentine's Day. In an 1862 copy of *Harper's Weekly* there is the following advertisement aimed at battle-weary soldiers who wished to remember their ladyloves:

SOLDIERS' VALENTINE PACKET
Price 50 cents
Containing

1 superb Valentine . . . . retail price	*25 cents*
1 elegant embossed Envelope	*3 cents*
1 elegant embossed Valentine	*6 cents*
3 comic Valentines	*9 cents*
1 beautiful Valentine Card in fancy Envelope . .	*6 cents*
3 white envelopes	*2 cents*

Tender messages lie hidden in the envelope pasted to this frilly valentine.

A sentimental bargain—unless one wonders how many lady sweethearts each soldier was supposed to have at home!

Even on the rough frontier, a wedding was a time for as extravagant an entertainment as could be arranged. In 1806, when Abraham Lincoln's parents were married in Kentucky, Thomas Lincoln wore silk suspenders to hold up his new black pants. The bride's gown had trimming of a quarter yard of scarlet cloth, a gift from the bridegroom. The "infare," or wedding feast after the ceremony was worth one guest's remembering:

> *We had bear meat, venison, wild turkey and ducks, eggs wild and tame, maple sugar lumps tied on a string to bite off for coffee or whiskey, syrup in big gourds, peach and honey, a sheep barbecued whole over coals of wood burned in a pit, and covered with green boughs to keep the juices in . . .*

Country square dances were just as gay, but they were also strenuous. A self-taught fiddler accompanied the sets with the same "Turkey in the Straw," "Arkansas Traveler," and "Old Zip Coon" that we know today. A caller half-sang, half-shouted, "Dip to your partner," "Dozy-do!" "Sashay right!" and "Swing her down the middle!" But it was not just the young folks who knew how to dance. An announcement in a copy of the Hartford *Courant* in 1860 said:

Not only for Bostonians, but for all Americans July 4th was a day for celebrations, usually noisy.

. . . The Old Folks will show the juveniles how to cut the pigeon wing at Union Hall tonight. If you don't believe it, drop in and see for yourself.

There were some religious groups, though, that thought dancing a sin and the fiddle an instrument of the devil. Young people in those groups, however, still managed to have fun. They invented the "play-party," which was a cross between dancing and the singing games of little children. In it there was much choosing and stealing of partners, and "figures" in which the couples swung each other by the hands, not by the waist. Kissing games were great favorites. Thus, if one's conscience approved, dancing of one sort or another could be enjoyed at all levels of society.

Manners in City Society

City society was, of course, much more formal than that of countryside and frontier. City folk tried in their dress, manners, speech, and parties to imitate the older societies of London and Paris. Social leaders were stung by the criticism of European visitors that the United States was too rough and crude a nation to be taken seriously by the civilized world. Such a critic as Mrs. Frances Trollope, a visiting Englishwoman, wrote about the "dull and heavy conversation," no words of which were spoken "with charm and grace." Of an evening party in Cincinnati she reported:

> *The gentlemen spit, talk of elections and the price of produce, and spit again. The ladies look at each other's dresses till they know each pin by heart; talk of Parson Somebody's last sermon on the day of judgment, on Dr. T'Otherbody's new pills for dyspepsia, till the "tea" is announced . . . It always appears to me that they remained together as long as they could bear it, and then they rise en masse, cloak, bonnet, shawl, and exit.*

Snowballing on Boston Common in 1856.

Mrs. Trollope's own manners might be questioned, for writing so contemptuously of her host country. However, she would have laughed aloud had she been present on one occasion when society and frontier met. This was at a ball in Springfield, Illinois, when the young lawyer, Abe Lincoln, asked to be presented to the visiting lady, Miss Mary Todd. The record says (and it is the kind of story he may have told on himself) that his first words to her were, "Miss Todd, I want to dance with you in the worst way." After a painful turn around the ballroom floor, the young lady, referring to his wish, said, "Mr. Lincoln, you have achieved your ambition." Here a backwoods boy, unschooled in the social graces, had met a young woman of fashion from Lexington, Kentucky. Such contrasts were to be found all over America in the nineteenth century.

Still, the elaborateness of some of the receptions, "levees," and balls of the day would take our breath away. There was the gala ball given in Boston to support the Greek nation in its 1824 fight for independence. So lavish were the decorations, so brilliant the lighting of many chandeliers, so gorgeous the gowns of the ladies at this event, that Boston newspapers declared themselves unequal to describing it.

On another occasion, also in Boston, the Prince of Wales had thrown the city's society into transports of delight with his royal presence. *Frank Leslie's Weekly* reported that sixteen hundred guests attended the soiree

Screened by tents, sportsmen try to spear eels through pond ice.

given in the young man's honor and described the dazzlingly ornate gowns of some of the lady guests. Crowded though they were, perhaps overelaborate, and to our tastes too stuffily formal, these great parties showed how far America had come from the days when it was a colony on the edge of the wilderness.

Exhibitions—Animal and Human

Our ancestors had an insatiable appetite for staring at the strange and the weird. Tamed or caged wild animals were favorite attractions. Early records tell of fur-trappers who sometimes caught and tamed a bear and brought it back, led on a chain, to civilization. They then made an easy penny at village taverns by showing the creature clumsily dancing and begging for its supper at its master's bidding.

Now and then a sailor just back from a long voyage appeared on a village green with a monkey on his shoulder. Sometimes its owner played a hurdy-gurdy or hand organ to which children danced and sang, remembering to drop a penny in the monkey's cup. In time the hurdy-gurdy man with his monkey became a common sight on city streets.

In 1815, in the hope of making his fortune in a new way, a man named Hachaliah Bailey bought an elephant for $ 1000 and began exhibiting it up and down the countryside. Imagine the excitement it caused in places where not even pictures of elephants had ever been seen. Soon some of his neighbors joined Hachaliah as partners. They bought other animals and started a touring menagerie. By 1820, traveling animal shows were plodding up and down the East coast. There were zebras, ostriches, giraffes, perhaps a mangy lion or tiger, and often a rhinoceros advertised as a "unicorn."

Gradually owners began to train a few animals to perform tricks. Horseback-riding acrobats joined the show. The animals traveled in two or three cages on wheels, drawn by tired horses—a far cry from the elaborate circuses of later days. Still, to have had the red and yellow wagons draw up in the main square of a sleepy village must have been exciting for young and old.

Other showmen traveled with "dioramas." After paying his penny, the viewer was permitted to peep through a glass window in the back of an enclosed wagon and see the moving picture sequence of battles, ships on fire, and royal processions. The showman explained them as they moved slowly by. Today the diorama would seem rather tame to us.

Ballyhoo men and an occasional clown went ahead of an exhibit to advertise its attractions and drum up trade. But town fathers sometimes refused to allow shows of any kind within village limits. It would be unwise, the selectmen thought, to let their simple village youths be influenced by the wild fellows who traveled with exhibitions. Also, they argued, factory girls and apprentices would be tempted to spend their few pennies foolishly "for these nonsenses."

All Americans loved a fiddler.

"The Greatest Showman on Earth"

On New York City's Broadway there had long been a museum of "strange and marvellous sights;" but it was not a success until, in 1841, it was sold to a young showman from Bethel, Connecticut. The young man who bought the moldering old building and its dusty contents was Phineas T. Barnum, whose name would go down in American entertainment sometimes as "the greatest humbug," and sometimes as "the greatest showman on earth." Both were his own phrases; both were true.

Barnum was perhaps the first high-pressure salesman in America. He realized that to make a success of the museum he needed to polish up the old exhibits, buy some shining new ones, and then *advertise!* This he did. His first great success with the curiosity-hungry public was the "Fejee Mermaid." This was a stuffed monkey's head and torso sewed or glued to the body of a large, scaly fish. Of course this was "humbug," and most people knew it. But, as Barnum often said, "people like to be fooled," and this certainly seemed to be true when their favorite showman, Phineas T. Barnum, did the fooling. Barnum's American Museum fast became the most popular place of amusement in New York City—so popular that some people stayed all day. This would never do, so the clever Barnum put up a new sign over a doorway; it said, "To the Egress." Thinking this was some strange animal, most people passed through the door, only to find themselves out in the street! For "egress" means, of course, "to go out."

Merrymaking at a wayside inn.

One of Barnum's greatest successes, however, was not a fake but the real thing—a midget, named "General" Tom Thumb. At the age of four the "General" was only 25 inches tall and weighed just 15 pounds. He very soon became a great favorite of the public, and both he and Barnum became rich men. With his fortune Tom built a miniature house for himself, with everything scaled to size. Barnum, equally in character, built himself a Persian palace called "Iranistan." Barnum even took General Tom Thumb and his miniature bride, Lavinia, to the White House where, at a brilliant reception, Mr. and Mrs. Lincoln shook hands with the tiny couple.

By mid-nineteenth century Phineas T. Barnum decided to jump on the traveling circus bandwagon and begin sending his famous curiosities, both animal and human, from one end of America to the other. One would expect this showman to have something new and startling up his sleeve. The "something new" was the largest tent ever dreamed of. So was born the modern circus.

Other circus managers ran Circus Boats up and down the great river highways of the nation. This was much simpler than packing a circus into tight wagons and taking a caravan cross-country over the impossible roads of the times. Some of the boats were known as "Floating Palaces." One on the Wabash River in 1853 was as lavish in its furnishings as the most luxurious city theater. The price of admission was the extravagant sum of fifty cents. Circus tickets were usually twenty-five cents.

In 1855, the steam calliope was patented by its inventor. Thereafter, rigged on the hurricane deck of a circus river boat, the "steam piano," as it was called, accompanied all the natural excitement of a circus with brassy, ear-piercing music. Incidentally, it almost cooked the poor "musician" who performed on the intensely steam-heated instrument.

Citified Entertainments

One of the strangest entertainments that otherwise sophisticated city people enjoyed was a mechanical "Turkish gentleman." It was advertised as being able to beat any possible human opponent at the popular game of chess. Its inventor made a great deal of money on gullible chess players until the hoax was discovered—a human chess wizard had been concealed behind the machinery. It had been an almost-Barnum story.

Securely roped and raised by a windlass, an elephant is hoisted on a ship bound for American shores.

Then as now, Americans loved to watch others perform daring feats.

Another city pleasure, horse racing, was popular in the Eastern metropolitan area from early in the nineteenth century. In 1814, a famous race on Long Island between horses named *American Eclipse* and *Henry* brought a purse of $20,000 to the winner, and more than $200,000 in bets changed hands that day. By midcentury, sailboat regattas were also attracting the well-to-do, as well as thousands of shoreline spectators, to the large seaside cities—again with much gambling as to possible winners. There were no organized sports as we know them. But in the 1850's a new game called "baseball" began to be enjoyed by young men and boys on the "Elysian Fields," a recreation park in Hoboken, New Jersey.

Boston boasted the first public city park in the United States—its Commons. Here Bostonians of an earlier century had turned their cows out to graze and had drilled their militia. Now it was a place where citizens strolled on balmy evenings; where little boys, in plush hats that looked like muffins, rolled their hoops; and where little girls, looking like miniature fashion plates, walked primly with their nursemaids. Lovers met here. Vendors peddled hot roasted oysters and chestnuts in season, and sold fresh gingerbread, spruce beer, molasses candy and lemonade.

In winter there was skating on the frozen park pond. Nathaniel Hawthorne described a traveling Show of Oddities that set up its booths on Boston Commons. It exhibited an enormous rat and a dancing bear. But it was the wax figures which really captured the public's imagination. There were pirates, murderers whose names had been in newspaper headlines, and Siamese twins—"admirably done, as natural as life"—so that many people were half convinced that the figures were the skins of real people, stuffed, and not wax at all. Sometimes on a summer night there was a firework display.

On sizzling summer days, it began to be the accepted thing to go sea-bathing, for the purpose of "enjoying the healthful benefits of salt water." Certainly very little sun touched the skins of either men or lady bathers, for both wore bathing suits that were as voluminous and all-enveloping as ordinary clothes. These were donned in "bathing machines," or tiny portable bathhouses pulled down to the very edge of the surf, so that there was no risk of exposing oneself in bathing dress to a curious public.

A revolutionary innovation was the daguerreotype, the earliest form of photography. At first glance, this invention in 1839 by a Frenchman, Louis Daguerre, may not seem like entertainment; but it certainly was. Imagine the excitement inspired by a machine that could, as people put it, "capture faces and trees and scenery and hold them in permanency." Here

The Great Barnum with Mr. and Mrs. Tom Thumb at left.

In the old Hippodrome on New York's Madison Square over a hundred horses, their riders dressed as knights, stage a tournament.

was a kind of magic brought about by the new science of chemistry. Its popularity took America as well as Europe by storm. Gone was the necessity of sitting tedious hours for a portrait painter or of having your face brushed into an already-painted figure by an itinerant portrait artist. Instead, you went to the Daguerreotype Studio where what we now call a photographer took your picture in a minute.

When Reading Scott was Daring

The American reading public still tended to read only that which was either highly moral or instructive in a practical way. In his *Autobiography,* Dr. Lyman Beecher tells of the struggle he had as a boy to persuade his father that "Bell's *Sermons,* Bogue's *Essays,* Bonnet's *Inquiry,* Toplady on *Predestination,* and the *State of the Clergy during the French Revolution*" did not completely satisfy a boy's longing for books with pith, excitement, and beauty. Dr. Beecher wrote:

> *In regard to Scott's novels, it will be remembered that, at the time they came out, novel writing stood at so low an ebb that most serious-minded people regarded novel reading as an evil.*

Such a thing as a novel was not to be found in our house. Great was the light and joy, therefore, when father spoke . . . "George, you may read Scott's novels. I have always disapproved of novels as trash, but in these is real genius and real culture, and you may read them." And we did read them; for in one summer we went through Ivanhoe *seven times, and were able both of us (Lyman and his brother) to recite many of its scenes, from beginning to end, verbatim.*

Almost until the twentieth century, most American writers had in mind the good of man's soul more than the creation of great literature. Most books were collections of sermons, travel journals, or biographies of men whose lives might inspire or instruct others. For this reason, many a fine young writer went unrecognized. In addition, books were expensive; few people had had more than an elementary education; and there were

Dressed from head to toe in bathing dresses of flannel, the ladies dare to submerge themselves at Coney Island.

almost no public libraries. Most of all, people had been so busy building a new nation that there had been all too little time and energy left for people to think of books. Still, the early nineteenth century saw the flowering of a native American literature. It was during Lincoln's lifetime that Hawthorne, Poe, Emerson, Thoreau, Longfellow, Mark Twain, and Walt Whitman lived and wrote. Bit by bit their countrymen would begin to read and to take pride in their writing.

From Fiddlers to Concert Stars

If literature was having a struggle to find its place in American life, the problems of music were even greater. Again it was the folk art aspect that was most favored. Americans everywhere liked a lively tune, fiddled by a play-by-ear musician. When asked for his musical opinions, Abraham

Lincoln wrote in 1860, "I will tell you confidentially that my greatest pleasure when taking a rest after splitting rails was to play a solo on the jew's harp."

The most popular composer of the period, Stephen Foster, borrowed or used Negro folk melodies as the basis for such songs as "My Old Kentucky Home," "Old Black Joe," "Massa's in de Cold Ground," and "Oh! Susanna!" These swept the nation because of their "folk" quality and their frank sentimentality. Love of the sentimental was the most conspicuous quality of America's popular musical taste. To supply fresh sheet music, not too difficult to play, to countless young women who had "taken piano lessons," publishers by 1864 were announcing titles such as: "Mother, Is the Battle Over?", "Angel Friends," "O, Ye Tears," "How Softly on the Bruised Heart," and "I'll Wait at the Gate for Thee."

In the homes of cultivated people of the South, of Eastern cities, and such new centers as Louisville, Kentucky, the music of Mozart, Handel and Haydn was played on chamber instruments like the violin and flute for a family's own pleasure or for that of their friends. Among such people it was customary to encourage young ladies to cultivate the slightest talent for singing or for playing the pianoforte. Making music—like painting china, reciting poetry, or doing fine embroidery—was thought to be a desirable social grace for a woman. As a result, a few trained musicians were able to earn a precarious living as teachers.

No matter how gifted a performer might be, there was little chance of his supporting himself by giving public concerts. For example, when Louis Gottschalk, born in New Orleans in 1829, was sent abroad to study piano, European musicians predicted a great musical career for the boy. But when he returned to his homeland in 1853, he discovered that New Yorkers "could stay away from his concerts in droves." In his *Notes of a Pianist,* he later wrote ruefully: "My first concert at New York was a success, but the receipts did not amount to one-half of the expenses. The second, given at Niblo's theatre, was a fiasco; in the two concerts I lost twenty-four hundred dollars." Years later the public was to flock to hear him; but not yet in midcentury.

In 1850, Phineas T. Barnum tried a bold experiment. He persuaded the "Swedish Nightingale," Jenny Lind, the toast of Europe, to brave the cultural wilderness of America. She was to sing a hundred and fifty concerts and receive the unheard-of sum of one thousand dollars for each. Her first concert took place at Castle Garden, the largest auditorium in New York. Tickets sold at auction for skyrocketing prices. The first one was bought by a hatter for $225. The next day every newspaper in the city carried the story, and from then on his hat shop did a record business! New York was conquered, as was every city up and down the Atlantic seaboard where Jenny Lind sang.

Charles Dickens, famous British novelist, gives a reading for an enthusiastic American audience.

If the photographer is to get a good daguerreotype likeness, the sitter must have his head held still in a clamp. Below: An advertisement from 1841.

There were other instances of interest in good music, but these were rare. The opera house in New Orleans established a remarkable reputation over a long period of time. Other attempts were less successful until the coming of large groups of German and Italian immigrants. With their ingrained love of good music, they demanded fine concerts and paid happily for them—not because it was fashionable to do so, but because they loved music.

DAGUEREOTYPE

PORTRAITS,

Taken with or without Sunlight, from ten o'clock, A. M. until dark, every day at the Studio of

PROFESSOR MORSE,

No. 136 Nassau Street,

Opposite the Brick Church, by

S. BROADBENT.

PROFESSOR MORSE, WILL GENERALLY BE IN ATTENDANCE.

N. B.—Portraits are taken equally well in *Cloudy*, and even in *Stormy* weather.

☞ More recently likenesses are taken in the sunlight in ONE SECOND of time; without the sun in TWENTY SECONDS.

ap17tf.

A Ticket to the Theatre

Drama also faced difficulties in the nineteenth century. For one thing, it was still felt that the theatre was somehow immoral. Actors and actresses were viewed with disapproval; boys and girls were warned against them. Still, there was something attractive about a play, particularly a melodrama. Many people could not resist the temptation to buy a ticket, even if it endangered their souls.

A young actor, Noah Ludlow, wrote in his autobiography of his difficulties in finding room and board while performing in Vicksburg, Mississippi: "The moment I said the word, 'theatrical,' I observed that she (the landlady) changed color. With a half-smothered voice she said, 'Theatre;' and then, with mock civility, 'I am sorry, sir, but I cannot accommodate you.'"

By the 1840's, small companies of actors were traveling up and down the country, moving seasonally, like migrating birds. Using the Mississippi River as a highway, they went to St. Louis in the summer, then south to New Orleans in November. Hair-raising melodramas were regular attractions on the Mississippi showboats. Even though the most respectable people did not attend plays and many religious groups disapproved of them as "spawning grounds of iniquity," there were six theatres in New York, all well-filled every night. Phineas T. Barnum avoided the disapproval of such visitors to his American Museum by calling his small theatre a "Lecture Room." Here he staged what he advertised as "refined amusements and moral dramas." It was even necessary to censor and change Shakespeare's plays before they could be performed or read before an American audience.

A fashionable opera dress of 1845.

Mrs. Trollope, the visiting Englishwoman, had something to say about the lack of manners displayed by Cincinnati playgoers in 1832:

> *The theatre was really not a bad one . . . but an annoyance infinitely greater than decorations indifferently clean, was the style and manner of the audience. Men came into the lower tier of boxes without their coats; and I have seen shirt sleeves tucked up to the shoulders; the spitting was incessant, and the mixed smell of onions and whiskey was enough to make one feel even the Drakes' acting dearly bought by the obligation of enduring its accompaniments . . . The noises, too, were perpetual . . . applause is expressed by cries and thumping with the feet, instead of clapping; and when a patriotic fit seized them, and "Yankee Doodle" was called for, every man seemed to think his reputation as a citizen depended on the noise he made.*

Abraham Lincoln liked the theatre. As everyone knows, it was while at a performance of the play, *Our American Cousin,* at Ford's Theatre in Washington on April 14, 1865, that he was shot by the half-crazed actor, John Wilkes Booth. The Civil War barely over, the president had agreed to spend an evening of much-needed relaxation, with Mrs. Lincoln and friends, in seeing a diverting play.

Apparently people went to the theatre in mid-nineteenth century only to see melodramas and thrillers. These served very much the same purpose as our early movies—a few hours of excitement, regardless of

An oyster stall does a brisk trade in the shadow of a theatre.

artistic quality. Serious drama was rare; American audiences were not eager for plays that had something of value to offer.

As we have seen, in the early nineteenth century America's pastimes, home life, industry, schools, and ways of travel were all in a state of rapid change. An adolescent, essentially rural United States was turning into a more mature, urban nation. Soon the crude pioneer way and the attempt to imitate European customs would fade. In their place would be something new to the world—the American way of life, much as we know it today.

In Village and Town

5

In Lincoln's America, life in a village was not so very different from life on a farm. Homes in the town were likely to be similar, inside and out, to those in the country except that the town house had a picket fence or a low stone wall around it and perhaps a footpath as a sidewalk outside its front window.

Some town houses, owned by sea captains or merchants, were handsome, two-and-three-story mansions. They often had fancy iron grillwork fences and delicate, fan-shaped windows, called fanlights, over a front door with a shining brass knocker. Such a home usually kept several servants or Negro slaves who lived in quarters behind the kitchen or in the attic. Its size and the richness of a home's furnishings depended, of course, upon the wealth of its owners. A well-to-do village merchant might have a handsome "banjo" clock, a set of Staffordshire china imported from England, a new wood-burning iron cookstove in his kitchen, a French mirror in a gilded frame hanging over a melodeon or small reed organ. The player had to pump this instrument frantically while his fingers pressed the keys, or no sound would come forth.

Part Farmer—Part Villager

Well-off or not, every village dweller had a large vegetable garden, a berry patch, and a few fruit trees at the back of his house. All of these needed tending by owner or hired man, as did the matched pair of horses in the carriage house and the milk cow in the stable. Sometimes even a few pigs were kept in the far corner of the lot, since it was good to have one's own fresh or home-cured meat.

The housewife, her daughters, and perhaps a hired girl were as busy as their farm sisters. There were milking, skimming, and churning to attend to; there were gooseberry pies to bake and fruit to preserve or turn into shining jelly. Fresh brooms must be made of new broomcorn, and clothes had to be boiled in tin tubs in the backyard, hung to dry, and later ironed with heavy flatirons heated on the stove. Chickens and geese from the backyard pen had to be fed, killed, plucked, dressed—then stuffed and roasted, or boiled until tender.

Younger boys carried wood and water endlessly; wood for stove and fireplaces (sometimes seven or eight in a single house), water for kitchen and horse trough. They drove the cow to pasture on the edge of the village

A lady milkman makes her rounds amid the bustle of a market town.

and led her home for milking. Their youngest sisters "minded" the baby or were set to cross-stitching samplers as a way of teaching them industrious habits and their alphabet at the same time. "Mottoes" were sentimental, such as "When this you see, remember me," or pious, like "The Devil makes work for idle fingers." At the bottom they embroidered their names, age, and the date they finished their samplers. How amazed those little girls would be to know that some of their faded handiwork still decorates the walls of their great-great grandchildren's homes.

The handiwork of their mothers is also treasured by many descendants. For skill with the needle was a highly esteemed nineteenth-century feminine talent. Beautiful crewel embroidery designs, stitched upon bed hangings and curtains, were often as artistically done as a painting. Intricate needlepoint designs were worked with patient, beauty-loving fingers, as were quaint, colorful quilt patterns.

Every villager—whether storekeeper, preacher, wheelwright, blacksmith, sea captain, miller, teacher, or doctor—was also part farmer and part householder. Even when he had become a busy lawyer and circuit court judge, Abraham Lincoln helped his wife, Mary Todd Lincoln, with the home chores. He pumped water from the cistern, kept the woodbox filled, milked the cow, curried his own horse. Then he washed his hands

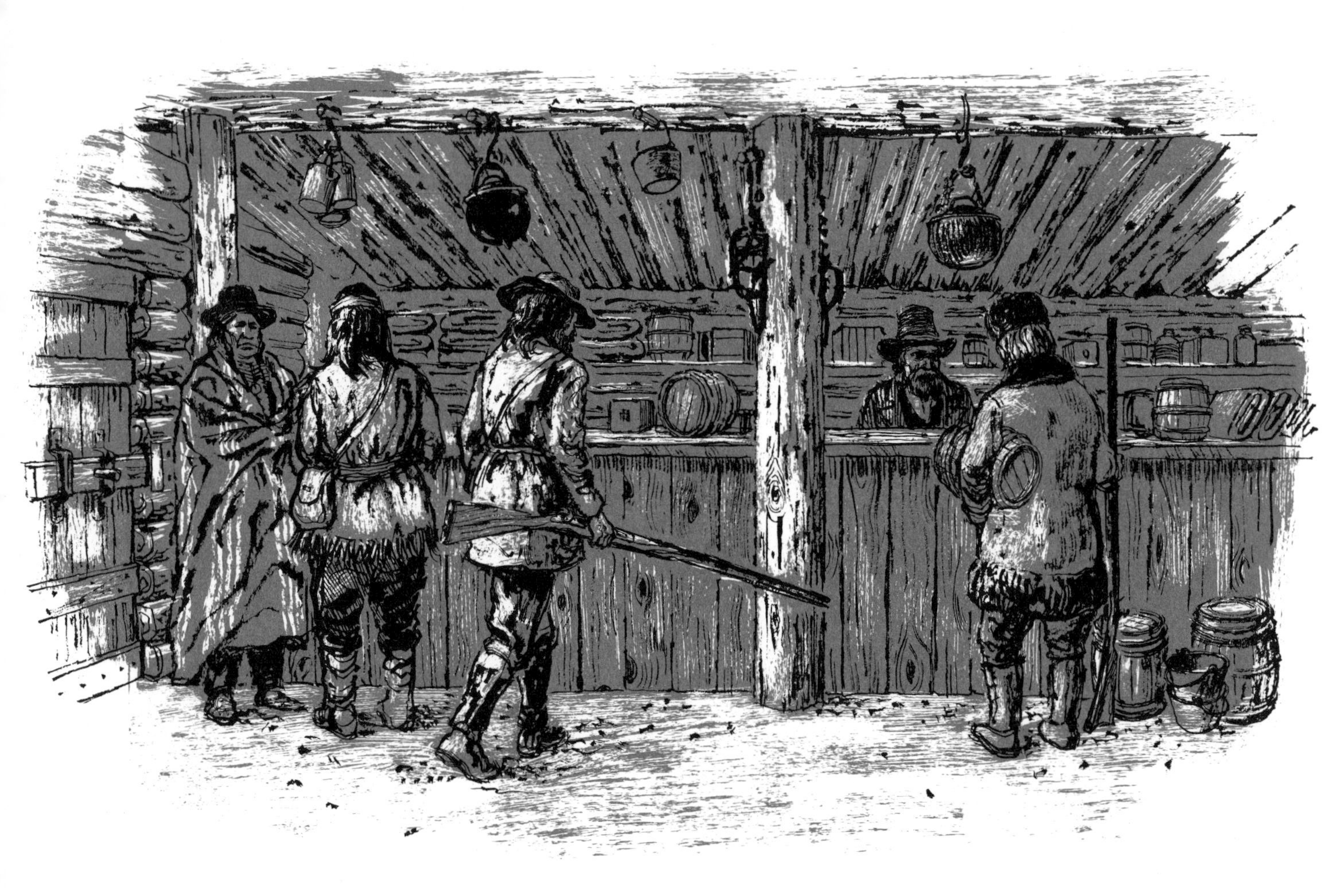

The counters of Western trading posts were high enough to hide the pistols worn by the clerks. Below: A steel-bladed axe.

with his wife's homemade soap in water poured from a china pitcher into a bowl set on a washstand. At bath time the Lincolns, like everyone else took turns in a huge tin tub set before the stove in the kitchen, bathing in water poured from steaming kettles.

The Lincolns' first home cost $1500 in 1843. It was in Springfield, Illinois, then only a village of about a thousand people. They moved into their next house soon after their first son, Robert Todd, was born. It was a story-and-a-half house, painted a light "Quaker" brown. Probably the Lincolns had lightning rods put on the four corners of their house, for this newfangled invention was something that people were excited about. Would those insignificant metal rods really send the tremendous voltage of a lightning streak into the ground, as the inventor claimed? Or might they attract the lightning and make fire even more likely? It was a serious question of the day.

As Lincoln saw it in 1837, Springfield was, according to Carl Sandburg, a thriving market town with nineteen dry goods stores, six churches, eleven lawyers, and eighteen doctors. There were carriages in which rode men dressed in ruffled shirts and ladies in fashionable silks and lace. Farm women, who had recently gone barefoot, now wore shoes on market day; their menfolk sported rawhide boots instead of homemade moccasins. The streets were a bedlam: carriages dashed by, wagon axles creaked, drivers yelled at steers, whips cracked. Hogs wallowed in knee-deep mud; wagonloads of farm produce lumbered past curious onlookers. This was no "one-horse-town," but it was not as "civilized" as might be thought—in 1836 a bounty of fifty cents was still being offered for "wolf scalps with the ears thereon."

Some new villages of the nineteenth century deliberately patterned themselves after the prim New England towns of a hundred years earlier. That is why even today there are villages in Ohio and Indiana with trim houses built around an elm-shaded green, with a steepled church at one end, and a tavern at the other. Some towns sprang up haphazardly, but there was usually a good, practical reason for their location. Maybe it was a crossing of two important Indian traces, or trails. Or perhaps there was a river that would be a natural highway for commerce and travel. Later, villages often sprang up at intervals of a day's journey by stagecoach along a turnpike.

To the first cabin or two was added a trading post, which later developed into a country store. This naturally attracted settlers. Then came meeting house, saw and grain mills, and a school. These strung themselves out on both sides of the turnpike, which almost always became known as "Main Street" in every American town. At first, a settlement held only farmers of the log cabin variety, a few fur trappers, and a post trader. When it began to thrive, the village attracted preacher, schoolteacher, doctor, lawyer, blacksmith, apothecary, cobbler, innkeeper, tavern keeper, tanner, even sometimes a hatter.

Hand-forged beaver trap, 1840. Below: An oak keg used for storing liquor or molasses, 1820.

Cracker Barrel and Pot-Bellied Stove

Abe Lincoln knew primitive frontier villages long before he knew the more citified Springfield of his married life. When a young man in New Salem, Illinois, he had been storekeeper's helper for fifteen dollars a month and a room to sleep in. Here he had stretched his six feet four inches to reach all sorts of merchandise for the customers: bombazine for a lady's dress, leather saddles, new razors and rifles, tall beaver hats for those men who aspired to be gentlemen, field hoes, kegs of "corn juice," or whisky, which he himself never drank.

As villages like New Salem grew into towns, more goods were added to the country store's wares: gold-washed breastpins for the ladies, whalebone corsets, coffee beans ready to grind at home, refined white sugar, jackknives, hoarhound candy drops and licorice sticks, and soda crackers that were counted from their barrel and weighed in old-fashioned scales. Most storekeepers did more business by barter than for money. Beaver and mink skins, butter and eggs were passed across the counter in exchange for salt, gunpowder, or whale oil. Chickens were sold at twelve to sixteen cents a pound. But "cash money" was scarce and "many a one parting with a silver dollar would squeeze it so hard the eagle would holler."

Besides being the source of good things to buy, the village store became

A glimpse of Brooklyn's past.

the social center, almost a clubhouse, for many townspeople. Here the men gathered when their day's work was done. They pulled up cracker and flour barrels close to the red-hot, pot-bellied stove and exchanged the latest village gossip, political and religious opinions, tales of marauding wolf or catamount, Indian fears, or news just brought from Eastern cities by stagecoach passengers.

The village store was often also the United States Post Office. Abe Lincoln was appointed Postmaster at New Salem in 1833. There, the mail came only twice a week—at first by horseback rider, later by stage. The writer of a letter penned it painstakingly on one side of a piece of paper with a turkey quill pen dipped in India ink or pokeberry juice. This he folded and sealed with a drop or two of red or green beeswax. Envelopes were unheard of. Since the person who received a letter had to pay for the postage at a rate which increased with the distance, a considerate friend would keep his letters as brief as possible. What young Lincoln enjoyed most was being allowed to read all newspapers that passed through his hands. His pay was some fifty dollars a year.

Honorable Fire Societies

Early fire buckets, made of leather, were decorated with allegorical paintings of fair ladies as well as the fire brigade's name.

There was one danger besides that of the Indian-on-the-rampage which all villages feared in the early nineteenth century—fire. In the days before modern fire engines, it was tragedy enough for a lonely farmhouse and its barns to go up in smoke and flames; but it was even worse to know that if your neighbor was careless with his candle or lamp, your home and those of all your friends might also be destroyed. True, in most towns there was a hand-operated fire engine, but it was still more of a toy than a help in time of need.

Gradually, groups of neigbors, who agreed to go to each others' aid at any hour of the day or night formed Fire Societies. In case of fire they formed a "bucket brigade" and exhausted themselves passing water, pail by pail, to the fire. Their members trained regularly, and it was the responsibility of each member to know the arrangement of other members' homes, especially the places where valuable china, silver, jewelry, books, and papers were kept. Membership was a badge of honor. The names of most famous men of the early nineteenth century can be found on faded lists of the Fire Societies of America's villages and towns. Between 1820 and 1830, fire insurance began to be offered for sale, but only rich men could afford such a luxury.

Leg-of-Mutton Sleeves and Beaver Hats

What a relief it must have been to village women in the early nineteenth century to find the shelves of every village store begin to be well stocked with bolts of ready-made cloth. But although the new mills meant that women need no longer spend long hours spinning and weaving, many garments still had to be cut and sewn by hand.

For years the housewife made her own patterns or borrowed them from a neighbor. But from 1828 on, the first women's monthly magazine in America, *Godey's Lady's Book,* gave the home seamstress aid and inspiration. Every village woman and girl longed not to look countrified in her dress. Here was the *Lady's Book* with illustrations in hand-tinted color, showing the "very latest Paris and New York fashions." Even more, it told how to cut patterns for the complicated overskirts, poke bonnets, leg-of-mutton and balloon sleeves, and boned waists. All women who could possibly afford it subscribed.

The new magazine also contained recipes for "hard" and "honey" soap and for boiling a tough Tom turkey—all phrased in the stilted, oversweet language of the time. But, without the reader's quite realizing it, her literary

A giant "shoe" hanging from an escape ladder or a swinging seat on a hoist carried fire victims to safety.

taste was also being developed. The lady editor, Mrs. Sarah Josepha Hale, often published, in serial form, the newest works of the leading writers of the day: Longfellow, Dr. Oliver Wendell Holmes, Whittier, Sir Walter Scott and Charles Dickens.

Most men of the time dressed soberly in tight trousers, swallow-tailed coats, and plain white broadcloth shirts. In cold weather they threw heavy capes or knitted shawls over their shoulders. Then, equipped with umbrella and, instead of brief case, a carpetbag, they were dressed for any sort of wind and weather. For Abe Lincoln, such a costume was a far cry from the buckskin trousers and linsey-woolsey shirt of his boyhood. Because he was so tall, his coats were usually too short, and so were his

The toy drum assures us that this is a boy.

pants. The fact that his shirt was often rumpled never bothered him. But he was very careful of his tall silk or beaver hat. To him and to other men of the time his hat was useful, not just ornamental. In it he kept his mail and many of his legal papers. Once he apologized to a friend for not having answered his letter. "I put it in my old hat," he said, "and buying a new one the next day, the old one was set aside, and so, the letter lost sight of for a time."

Folk Artists

Unhappily, the "fine arts" of painting, sculpture, and music (as perfected through centuries of study and effort in Europe) received all too little attention in a young America that was bursting at its seams with trying to "get ahead." But here, too, the people's desire to make their homes beautiful created some opportunity for a few men with varying degrees of artistic gifts to earn a living at unschooled, or what is known as "primitive," art.

Even though a housewife might long for the handsome French or Chinese wallpapers that were being brought to our shores by clipper ship, the slenderness of her purse often prevented her from satisfying this wish. However, she could and often did hire an "artist" to paint a mural on the wall over her fireplace: a pastoral or Biblical scene, a sleighing party, or an Indian peace council, complete with pipe. In one New England house, built in 1825 and still lived in, there is what seems to be dining room "wallpaper." Some forgotten artist painted the same ochre-yellow tulip design set in a geometric figure over the entire plaster wall. One wonders for what price he undertook so boring a task. Other artists achieved almost the same wallpaper effect by transferring a stenciled woodcut design to all wall surfaces.

There was, too, a great demand for portraits. To have a gilt-framed painting of himself hung in his parlor was a sign to acquaintances that a man was successful. There was a more far-reaching benefit. Were it not for these portraits, prized today in many of our own homes, how would we know how our great-great-grandparents looked? To answer this need, many a young man with a horse and wagon, a few brushes and paints, and a bit of a gift for catching a likness on canvas, chose the life of an itinerant portrait painter. He could travel only in summer when the roads were passable. But he very cleverly spent his winters painting canvasses for next season's possible customers. Then, in June he could pull from his wagon the almost-completed portraits of a sturdy farmer dressed in his Sunday-go-to-meeting broadcloth suit, and of his wife in her best black bombazine dress. All the painter needed to do was to paint in their faces!

In the height of fashion.

If there were children in the home, he would produce an already-pictured boy of approximately the age of the son of the house, with an appropriate dog, toy wagon, or fishing rod in the background. If a girl, her model would be holding a doll or a tiny nosegay. Because clothes for boys were as beruffled as those for girls, such a toy was often the only clue to the sex of the child. An old account book shows that at least one man paid the itinerant painter the munificent sum of $2.92 for a portrait of his daughter.

City Life

6

Nineteenth century American cities would seem only quaint and charming towns to us today. Still, Boston, New York, and Philadelphia were great cities in the opinion of their proud citizens. In 1820, there were 60,000 people in Boston; by 1840, there were 300,000 in New York. They were both centers of trade and shipping.

Compared to life in outlying settlements or small towns, here were excitement and bustle: a big fire, a robbery, a runaway horse; drays, carriages and coaches clattering down the main streets; a man walking up and down wearing sandwich boards advertising "Dr. Schenck's Mandrake Pills for diseases of the liver;" a new store going up that would sell nothing but toys! For the socially ambitious, New York and Boston were the centers of a new nation that still aped the manners and fashions of London and Paris. For the young man with energy, zeal, or a dream of his own, the city beckoned with hundreds of exciting possibilities.

Fan-shaped Windows and Lace-like Balconies

What did they look like, these cities? In the better residential streets there was the solid block of row-houses, built of brick. In Philadelphia and Baltimore, many had white marble doorsteps which were scrubbed every morning until they glistened. Some entrances had ornate iron railings and grillwork with beautiful fanlights over their doorways. Homes of well-to-do citizens might be of brick, as much as three stories high, with large windows and shining white shutters. In New Orleans there were lacelike grillwork balconies leaning over the streets.

Inside, many of these city homes had spacious rooms, wide staircases, elegant, often ornate furnishings, heavy window draperies, imported carpeting, and much bric-a-brac. Some householders had discovered that designers were making lovely furniture here in the United States. These people were buying custom-made desks, tables, and chairs from the young Duncan Phyfe who had lately opened a workshop and salesroom in New York. American-made clocks, by Seth Thomas of Connecticut, were also becoming popular; some had alarms, others chimes.

Farther from the center of the city, residential streets looked much like those of a village. Here houses were more widely separated; their trim

No elegant service here, but at least the townswomen could be sure of fresh fish.

yards with grass and ornamental trees and shrubs were enclosed by wooden fences or brick walls. The fences were there for good reason, since pigs were allowed to roam the streets at will. Charles Dickens wrote of a street scene in New York in 1842:

> *Two portly sows are trotting up behind this carriage, and a select party of half a dozen gentlemen hogs have just now turned the corner . . . They are never attended upon, or fed, or driven or caught, but are thrown upon their own resources in early life, and become . . . knowing in consequence.*

He might have added geese and chickens, for these, too, were not always penned by their owners—even in the best of neighborhoods. As one writer said, Americans, even city dwellers, were still farmers at heart. City backyards were often large enough for a vegetable patch, a henhouse, a few fruit trees, and flowers. There was also a backyard outhouse, for of course no home, however well-to-do, had piped running water or a bathroom.

A visitor to Boston in 1820 marveled at the honesty of its people. He was astonished to see that loaves of baker's bread, uncovered crocks of fresh milk, and the morning paper, left on every doorstep by a delivery

As a startled lady scurries to safety, a Boston policeman, in top hat, dashes forward to halt the reckless coachman.

JONES SHREVE BROWN
226
JONES BALL & COMPY

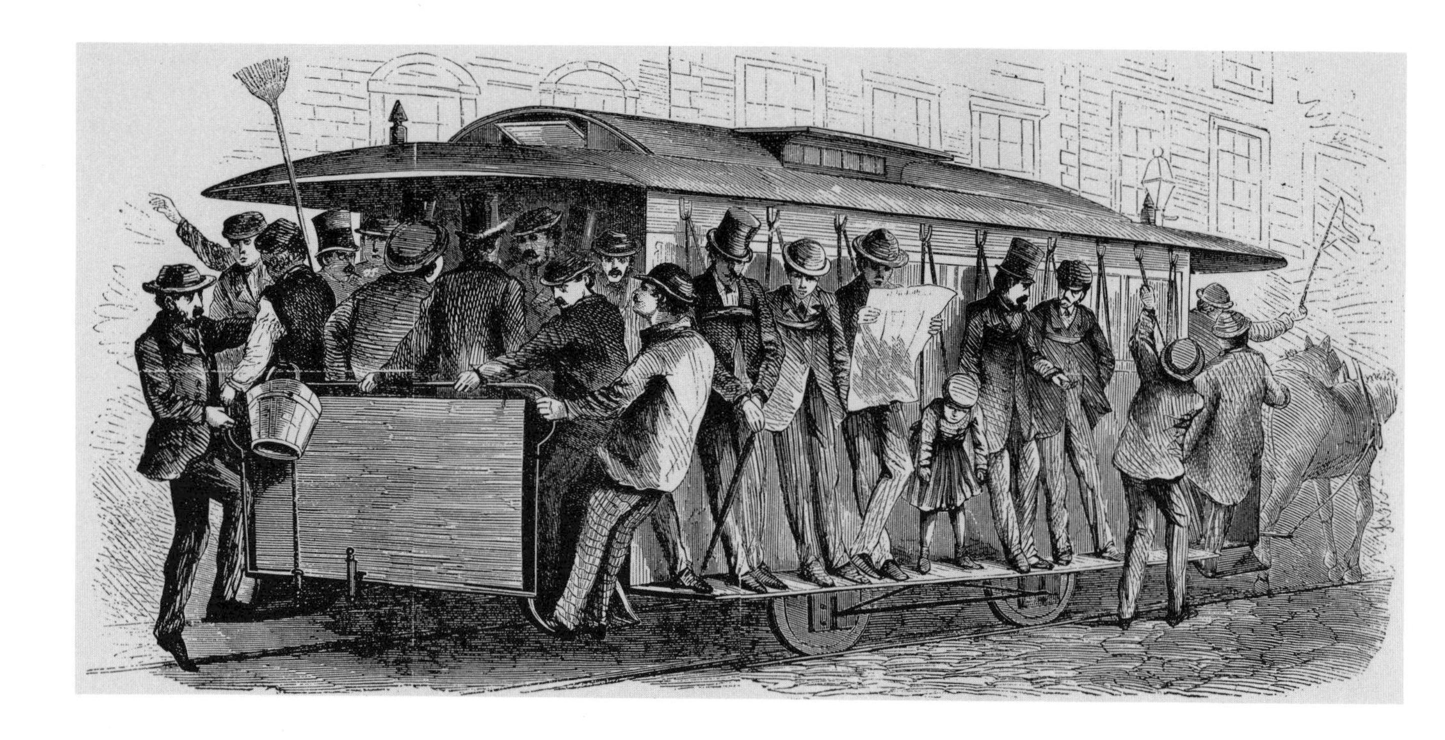

Room for one more on a New York streetcar.

boy, were unmolested until maid or housewife took them in. Later in the morning the bell of the meat wagon brought housewife or maid running to the street. This butcher's shop on wheels made daily stops at customers' houses.

Gingerbread, Oysters, and Succotash

Food for city dinner tables came from farms and dairies of the surrounding countryside. It was peddled up and down the streets by farmers and hawkers who tempted housewives with such cries as: "Gingerbread—hot from the oven!", "Oysters to melt in your mouth!", "Chestnuts! Don't burn your fingers!", and "Fresh violets for your sweetheart!" Little old ladies sat on street corners selling apples. At seaside towns there was a harvest of clams, oysters, and fresh fish to offer—some ready to eat. By the turn of the nineteenth century, open stalls in Northern markets were selling chestnuts, peaches, pears, rhubarb, sweet corn, cauliflower, eggplant and head lettuce. In the South the stalls also offered cantaloupe, raw peanuts, and watermelon. On most city tables "rye-and-Injun bread" was still everyday fare, with brown sugar and sorghum molasses for sweetening. White bread and refined sugar were expensive rarities, brought out along with imported China tea, only for special guests. A delicacy the Indians had taught Americans to prepare was succotash, a savory mixture of tender lima beans and corn, simmered in cream.

We would laugh today at some of the old wives' notions about food that were taken seriously:

> *The potato, nutritive and harmless as it appears, belongs to a family suspected of very dangerous traits. It is a family connection of the deadly nightshade and other ill-reputed gentry, and sometimes shows strange proclivities to evil. Scientific directors, bid us beware of the water in which potatoes are boiled,—into which, it appears the evil principle is drawn off.*

A woman's magazine was even fearful of the innocent and nutritious raisin. In its pages an editorial said:

> *It has been noticed that several children have died from convulsions produced by eating the skins of raisins. Dr. Dewees, of Boston, mentions the deaths of three children from this cause, and remarks that there is no stomach, unless it be that of an ostrich, that can master the skin of the raisin.*

One writer has left a record of a difficulty in transporting applesauce. His grandmother sent kegs of homemade applesauce every autumn to her children in the city. Almost invariably the boat bringing the treat downstream froze tightly in the river for four or five months. When it finally arrived in early spring, chunks were chipped off and thawed for the dinner table!

Sleighs and Surreys

There was no regular police force in Boston or New York until the 1840's. Instead, a few citizens were appointed to keep order. These wore badges but no uniforms. A watchman still walked up and down the city streets crying the hours: "Twelve o'clock and a cloudy night. All's well!" It was he who shook his rattle and shouted "Fire! Fire!" to wake the volunteer firemen. Throughout the nineteenth century there were many terrible fires in the large American cities, and much disastrous property loss. Theatregoing was particularly risky, since there were no fire laws.

A fashionable carriage known as a Lady's Basket Pony Phaeton with Rumble.

Visitors came to the cities on horseback, by stagecoach, or by boat. Not until well into the century were rail lines laid. Then the noisy, smoking "teakettle-on-a-track" brought hardy travelers into the cities at the breathtaking speed of fifteen to twenty miles an hour. Seeing a new locomotive for the first time in 1839, one man wrote:

> *It's a great sight to see a large train get under way . . . As to the engine, the most pithy and expressive epithet I ever heard applied to it is "Hell-in-Harness." Just imagine such a concern rushing unexpectedly by a stranger-to-the-invention on a dark night, whizzing and rattling and panting, with its fiery furnace gleaming in front, its chimney vomiting fiery smoke above, and its long train of cars rushing along behind like the body and tail of a gigantic dragon—or like the d—l himself—and all darting forward at the rate of twenty miles an hour.*

Those people who lived nearby came to a city in their own wagon or chaise, a two-wheeled covered vehicle hung on a C-spring. Later there were buggies, surreys, and streetcars pulled on rails by horses.

City streets were alive with traffic. There were almost as many kinds of vehicles as there are automobiles today. Among them was the two-wheeled Boston chaise—popularly called the "shay"—with folding top to keep off sun and rain. There was also the cabriolet, a two-passenger vehicle invented in France. The curved shape of its body and its leather hood reminded people of the graceful lines of a nautilus shell. This became the favorite carriage for the fashionable man-about-town. The master drove the cabriolet himself, but there was a small outside rear seat for a groom, called "the tiger." When the master alighted, it was the tiger's job to jump off quickly and hold the horse until his master returned.

Making his nightly rounds, the lamplighter was a cheerful sight.

There were also hansom, or hackney, cabs which a visitor to the city might hire. (A few of these can still be seen in New York near the Plaza Hotel, waiting to take nostalgic people on a drive through Central Park.) For whole families there were various closed, four-wheeled coaches, the brougham being the most popular. The city family that could afford its own private coach also needed a coachman, a footman, and a groom to care for the horses and keep the vehicle shining. With ladies the so-called phaeton was the favorite carriage for paying calls and for shopping. Its seat was wide enough to allow skirts to spread without being crushed.

And there was the surrey, which sometimes did have a fringe on top. It was a family-sized, Sunday-go-to-meeting carriage, used like our "station wagon" automobiles. The first public carriage to follow a regular route was operated from Wall Street to Dry Dock in New York City in 1831. Others, called rockaways, soon began transporting passengers from the new railway stations to their hotels.

In winter, Northern city streets became even more colorful, for with the first snowfall a bewildering variety of sleighs appeared. As with wheeled vehicles, some of these were built large, low, and comfortable for

A "perambulating water cart" designed to keep down dust in hot city streets.

use by an entire family. Others were light, swift, and graceful to please the debonair and fashion-conscious.

It must have been fun on a frosty morning to be driven to school in a small, bright-red, two-passenger cutter, or in a sleigh shaped much like a carriage and set high on bob-runners. In either case, there were gaily tinkling bells attached to the horses' harness. Most sleighs were open, though some had folding tops in case of a snowfall. To ward off frozen toes and hands, passengers wrapped themselves in buffalo or bearskin rugs.

In 1842, streets were usually of cobblestone, on which horses' hooves made a great clatter. Looking down on Broadway from his room in Carlton House, Charles Dickens saw:

> *No stint of omnibuses—plenty of hackney cabs and coaches, too; gigs, phaetons, large-wheeled tilburies, and private carriages. Negro coachman and white; in straw hats, white hats, glazed caps, fur caps; in coats of drab, black, brown, green, blue, nankeen, striped jean and linen.*

He might have added that horses drawing a carriage might be wearing a net over their ears—both as decoration and as protection against flies.

Ladies of fashion choose fabrics from the well-stocked shelves of a dry-goods shop. Below: In 1859 Macy's was already offering bargains for the ladies.

NICE Laces at Macy's.
NICE Embroideries at Macy's.
NICE Hosiery and Gloves at Macy's.
NICE Linen Handkerchiefs and Corsets at Macy's.
NICE Linen Goods cheap at Macy's.
NICE Paris Flowers at Macy's.
NICE Paris Ribbons at Macy's.
NICE Housekeeping Dry Goods at Macy's.
NICE Joined Blond Edgings, 2 cents a yard.
NICE and CHOICE MAKE of
REAL **KID GLOVES**, 63 cents a pair.
204 and 206 Sixth Avenue, corner 14th Street.

Sidewalks were sometimes of planks, sometimes of brick; but this applied to main streets only. Complaining of the mud in a sidestreet in Boston, one writer said that "if you saw an aged man poking about in the mud with a cane, you were tempted to ask if anybody was missing." When streets were too dusty or muddy for a gentleman's taste, he often paid a strong boy to carry him across on his shoulders.

By 1840, New York was a busy, self-important metropolis. An Englishman visiting the city at that time observed that "the very carts, instead of being drawn by horses at a walking pace, are met at a gallop and always at a brisk trot." Broadway was a street to marvel at, three miles long, perfectly straight but with paving that was wretchedly uneven, and sometimes with holes deep enough to break an unwary horse's leg. Gas lights had recently been installed, though only enough to light the city street dimly. Each evening at dusk the lamplighter made his rounds; with torch in hand, he climbed his ladder and ignited the gas in each lamp. Another utility which we take for granted was water from barrels set on horse-drawn wagons and sold to householders who did not have their own wells.

Frivolous Fashions

Dry goods stores and shops in the cities were offering a bewildering array of things for sale. Newspaper advertisements spoke of "English, French, and India fancy and Staple Dry Goods at Wholesale and Retail." Also of "Merino Long and Square Shawls, Camel's Hair and other Rich and Desirable Shawls usually imported." One store, the George W. Warren & Co. in Boston, held occasional mark-down sales—America's first bargain days!

Just as today, shopping was a source of pleasure to ladies. It was customary for a gentlewoman to do her shopping between twelve and two o'clock. From his chair in the window of Carlton House, Charles Dickens described the show of fashion that promenaded up and down Broadway on a hot summer day:

> *Heaven save the ladies, how they dress! We have seen more colors in these ten minutes than we should have seen elsewhere in as many days. What various parasols! what rainbow silks and satins! what pinking of thin stockings, and pinching of thin shoes, and fluttering of ribbons and silk tassels, and display of rich cloaks with gaudy hoods and linings! The young gentlemen are fond, you see, of turning down their shirtcollars and cultivating their whiskers, especially under the chin; but they cannot approach the ladies in their dress or bearing.*

It disturbed many foreign observers to see how few gentlemen of fashion paraded with the ladies on city streets in America. Men—even rich men—seemed to be almost entirely devoted to business during daylight hours, as they still are.

A daring bloomer dress. Below: The salesman has no difficulty in tempting his fair patrons.

Ladies bought stockings, shoes, parasols, perfume, and smelling salts from the fashionable shops on Broadway, but their flounced and beruffled gowns and hoods were made to order. There were also bloomer costumes —introduced in 1851 by Amelia Bloomer, a writer and editor who fought

A scene in a New York police court was typical of life in the fast-growing cities.

for "women's rights"—intended for use by daring young ladies for cross-country walking and at the seashore.

Because the day of ready-made dresses was still far away, women engaged in an endless round of shopping for dress materials, trimmings, buttons, laces, French ribbons, and so forth. There were also straw bonnets handwoven in Florence, Italy, jet earrings, and veils. A slipper bag was necessary for party-going. Because of the muddy or dusty streets, a lady wore her everyday shoes on the way to a salon, then changed to her dainty satin or brocade slippers in her hostess's dressing room.

Few items of a lady's wardrobe were as important as her veils. These were worn for modesty in public, as well as for beauty's sake. They were also worn for reasons of health. *Godey's Lady's Book* warned: "If the wind is blowing, a veil should be worn over the face, at least of ladies and children; otherwise fatal inflammation of the lungs, 'pneumonia,' may take place."

Corsets, too, were extremely important to the lady who wished to have the approved hourglass figure. This, however, was a garment strongly disapproved of by some men, one of whom compared waltzing with a tight-laced young lady to "spinning around with a clothes prop." Just as important to a lady of fashion was the arrangement of her hair. This meant shopping for ornamental combs, nets, and "rats" of hair with which to puff out her natural tresses. Feathers were so highly in demand that the beautiful egret and the colorful native American parrot were almost entirely killed off to supply milady's wishes.

A lady did not wear rouge, or, if she did, would never confess to the deception. A little orris root powder dusted on the face was her only approved make-up.

Gentlemen, both young and old, cared almost as much as the ladies about their appearance. Their suits were of fine broadcloth, their vests of brightly colored felt trimmed with brass buttons. Shirt fronts were pleated or ruffled. They wore tall hats, sometimes of black silk, sometimes of white beaver. They carried thick gold pocket watches with a key for winding, and swung walking canes with a jaunty air. Whiskers and mustaches were as important to a man as a wasp waist to his lady. Much more than today, when men tend to dress alike, clothes "made the man." A stranger was judged by his manners, his speech, and his clothing, in that order.

In contrast to the gentleman, the city artisan could be recognized by the coarse, practical quality of his dress. His breeches were probably of yellow buckskin, his shirt checked. His red flannel jacket was made at home; and his slouch hat, cocked at the corners, was usually worn and discolored. His shoes, of neat's or calf skin, were decorated with large brass buckles. These buckles and his "leathern" apron also revealed that he was a carpenter, a livery stable keeper, a tinsmith, or a brick mason who was proud of his hard-learned trade.

Grog Shops and Taverns

On their way home from work, gentlemen and apprentices alike stopped at a tavern for a drink of the cheap beer or whisky which flowed by the

Needy folk combing through rubbish that has been dumped as land fill.

barrel from distilleries in every city and town. In New York the "Old Brewery" section at Five Points was a source of much depravity among the poor of the city for many years. Finally it was torn down and a Home Mission built on the site—its purpose to spread the Gospel. But even after the 1840's, when a city police force was established, this slum section of New York filled the courts with its bedraggled poor. After drinking too much beer and "grog" in the saloons found on almost every street corner, such people often ended up fighting with knives, bricks and clubs. For many laborers, immigrants and apprentices, the saloon was a kind of clubhouse, much like the country store in a village. Here they met friends for a card game, an evening of conversation and sometimes checkers.

Well-to-do gentlemen of influence and respectability stopped on their way home from the office at the "Public Ordinaries," or fashionable bars, which often occupied whole floors of hotels. Admission to these was by card or membership, as in a select club.

A novel mailbox built into a lamppost.

Servants and Apprentices

Housemaids and apprentices tried their best to dress and act like upper-class folk. Something in the independent character of an American never has relished being the servant of another man or woman. House servants were usually country boys and girls eager to make their fortunes in the city. Some were recent immigrants from England or Ireland. In neither case did the young men or women intend to remain servants for long. They preferred to be called "hired help," and often found it hard to learn "correct" serving manners.

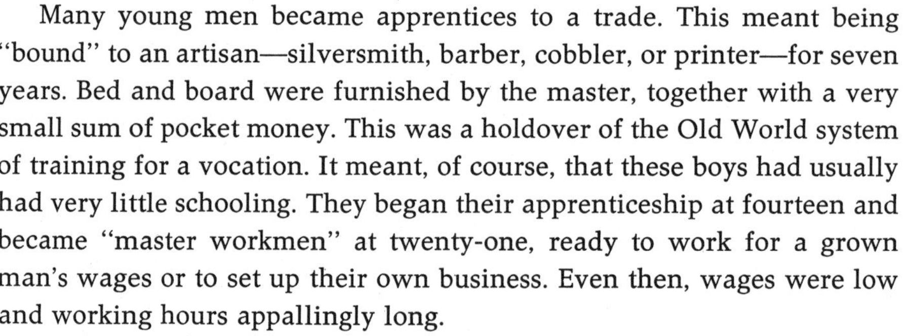

Many young men became apprentices to a trade. This meant being "bound" to an artisan—silversmith, barber, cobbler, or printer—for seven years. Bed and board were furnished by the master, together with a very small sum of pocket money. This was a holdover of the Old World system of training for a vocation. It meant, of course, that these boys had usually had very little schooling. They began their apprenticeship at fourteen and became "master workmen" at twenty-one, ready to work for a grown man's wages or to set up their own business. Even then, wages were low and working hours appallingly long.

The "Onion Place" Called Chicago

There was much vying with each other among the cities. A New York writer early in the century remarked that Boston seemed to feel that it was "special," more to be envied and imitated than any other American city. Particularly in their fine manners, cultural standards, and artistic tastes, Bostonians definitely considered themselves a superior breed.

But other cities were growing and becoming less and less like frontier towns. The Atlantic seaboard was not to remain the unrivalled center of

A raised wooden walk was helpful in a muddy Chicago street.

American life—though as late as 1830 many people, President Jefferson among them, believed seriously that it would be five hundred to a thousand years before the whole country would be settled and developed. By 1820, Lexington, Kentucky, was called "the most exciting place in the West." It boasted newspapers, schools (some free to the public), a college, a library, and excellent stores. This was where Mary Todd, later Mrs. Lincoln, was brought up as the pampered daughter of a leading citizen; here she wore dresses from Paris and drank her coffee from fragile English cups.

St. Louis, Missouri, the center of the fur trade, was by 1833 a cosmopolitan river city where traders, trappers, and immigrants were all settling. At first they came plodding overland in Conestoga wagons; later they chugged up the Mississippi River by steamboat from New Orleans. New Orleans itself had long been both an important shipping center and a city with a French population that gave it an exotic Old World flavor.

As late as 1820, Chicago was still a frontier post, with no sign that it would some day be one of the greatest cities in the United States. People still remembered that its Indian name had been "Chicagou," or "onion place." For longer than the memory of white man or red, the flat plain on which the town stood had been pink every spring with the blossoms of wild onions. By 1833, Chicago's population was only three hundred and fifty souls, though already it was a transfer place for lake steamers loaded with westward-moving people, barrels of flour grown and milled in the Middle West, lumber and furs. By 1847, it had grown so lustily that it

Not ancient Egypt, but the nation's capital at the time the Washington Memorial was being built.

could play host to the Whig River and Harbor Convention, which Abe Lincoln attended. Hotels were so overcrowded with out-of-town visitors that many people slept on ships docked in the harbor. Some even camped in the streets. The convention itself was held in a giant tent. Chicago was already on its way to becoming a center of Western railroads and industry. Even the Great Fire in the 1870's interrupted Chicago's growth only fleetingly and gave it an opportunity to rebuild its first flimsy buildings more sturdily. Those first wooden shacks, its citizens now realized ruefully, had been an invitation to fire.

Farm Boy in the City

Ever since the world's first city, there have been boys from the country who have been attracted to the big town by the bright lights, the excitement and the hope of making a fortune. In the early days of the 1800's, most of the farm boys who came to the city became apprentices to a trade. Later, like their sisters in the spinning mills, most of these took jobs in factories, as the handmade product gradually became machine-made.

One such young man was Peter Cooper. Apprenticed to a carriage maker, he came to New York already the inventor of several crude machines of his own. To avoid the dull work of pounding dirty clothes in a barrel of soapy water—the same dreary chore performed once a week by thousands of groaning boys all over the country—Peter had concocted a washing machine for his mother. Because he was ill at ease socially and felt keenly his lack of education, Peter Cooper did not dress up and wander around the city streets with other apprentices at night and on Sundays. Instead, he worked away at other inventions.

Peter Cooper went on inventing machines of one kind or another all his life. It was he who built the tiny "Tom Thumb" locomotive with a top speed of eighteen miles an hour, the locomotive famous for its race with a horse. He eventually made a vast fortune in the Horatio Alger tradition

The unfinished Capitol looms over the wintry Washington scene.

—by turning the two thousand dollars he had invested in a glue factory into a multimillion dollar business.

What was even more important was that he remembered the embarrassment of being an awkward apprentice with no education. He saw the hordes of young men and women attracted to the factories of the burgeoning city of New York. Many were living in ill-heated, miserably dark and dirty rooms; for as America's cities grew, so did her slums. With long working hours and poor pay, they had little hope of bettering their lot. Peter Cooper resolved to help them; so, in 1859, he established the Cooper Union for the Advancement of Science and Art. It was open at night for any young man or woman of the city. There was no age limit and no tuition fee. The school offered courses in chemistry, physics, mathematics, music, drawing and clothing design. There was, besides, a free public reading room—the only one in New York. One observer wrote of the first registration day: "There was a mob assembled so large and eager that the efforts to register students almost resulted in a riot. It was incredible that there should be such a passion for learning among the toilers."

It was at Cooper Union, in February, 1860, that Abraham Lincoln made one of his most famous speeches—a speech that helped make him President later that same year.

A White House reception was a very formal occasion.

The Backwoods Capital

When Abigail Adams arrived in Washington in 1800 to join her husband, the new President, she found the young capital to be a "city" in name only. Virgin forests had just been cleared from the bank of the Potomac River. A French engineer, Major L'Enfant, had laid out what would some day be Pennsylvania Avenue. It had not yet been cleared of all its tree stumps. One wing of the Capitol building was ready for Congress to use; meanwhile, what is now the impressive dome was a gap, open to rain and snow.

Nearby there were clusters of log cabins without glass windows, some workmen's shacks, crude stores and a few blocks of new brick row-houses. Owners of these homes took in Congressmen for room and board during the months when Congress was in session. Unfortunately, the red clay soil of Washington became fine dust in dry weather and liquid cement in rain. Mosquitoes in this swampy lowland spread malaria among all new Washingtonians, so that the city's population was alternately burning with fever or shivering with malarial ague. No wonder foreign diplomats called Washington "squalid," "backwoods capital," or "wilderness city."

Life in the Unfinished White House

At the other end of Pennsylvania Avenue, the handsomely designed White House was still being worked on. Here the Adamses lived in the six

A "fly front, over sack" of the 1860's.

completed rooms. When Mrs. Adams arrived, there was not a single bell in the immense house; nor were there any plans for a bell system! She also worried about the cost of the many candles it would take to light the mansion, for this was an expense which would come out of her husband's pocket. Hearth fires for the coming winter were her greatest concern. Surrounded by forest though the city was, firewood was almost impossible to buy, even at a high price. After all, there was a nation's capital city to build. Nor had anyone given any thought to the matter of drying laundry. So Abigail Adams wrote her daughter that since "We have not the least fence, yard, or other convenience . . . the great unfinished audience-room I make a drying-room of, to hang up the clothes in."

Finally completed in 1818, the new White House was still a far cry from the mansion we now automatically expect a President to have. Despite hickory wood fires in every room, it was drafty and gloomy and almost impossible to make into a livable home. Guests at state balls complained that they almost froze. It was still lighted by oil lamps and chandeliers of many candles until 1848, when gas fixtures were first installed. Even so, at the next state reception, when the newfangled gas lights flickered out, guests and President were glad to have the old-fashioned wax candles lighted, one by one.

Until 1850, all the food served at the table of the White House was prepared over an enormous open fireplace crowded with old-fashioned cranes, pots, hooks, and hand-turned spits. When the first "cook stove" was introduced in the kitchen, it so frustrated the cooks that there was real danger of President Fillmore going hungry. Finally he himself paid a visit to the United States Patent Office to find out how to work the new contraption.

Social decorum was a genuine problem in both the White House and the city of Washington. Every nation of the civilized world watched eagerly to see how the new "Republic" would behave. For instance, would Washingtonians, having no special privileges of birth, observe the rules of social precedence at White House parties: certain ambassadors on the President's right; others on his left, etc.? President Jefferson said "No." He established what came to be called the "rule of pell-mell." "All persons," he said, "when brought together in society are perfectly equal, whether foreign or domestic, titled or untitled, in or out of office." After they had entered the State Dining Room, the guests were to sit wherever they chose around a democratically round table. This practice so upset the British minister to Washington, Sir Anthony Merry, that he never again appeared at a White House party. This same dignitary had already been outraged when he had paid a formal call on President Jefferson in full gold lace, uniform, and dress sword, only to be received by the First Citizen of the United States in slippers and untidy morning dress.

In pictures taken on the day the Lincolns came to Washington as President and First Lady in 1861, the new leader of his country looks as loose-jointed and awkward as ever. His long arms dangle from his new black broadcloth coat sleeves; the swallow-tail of his coat is, as usual, not quite long enough. He is wearing three new jet shirt buttons set in silver, for which he paid fifty cents each. But his shirt and vest are rumpled. Set straight on his head is a new tall silk hat. The social crudeness of this frontier President contrasted sharply with the sophistication of some of his predecessors.

The new President Lincoln hated formality and show. He was determined not to be bound by social fiddle-faddle. So it was that he blacked his own boots and was more than once discovered sewing a button on his coat. Several important visitors found him pacing his study at night, dressed in an old-fashioned yellow flannel nightgown and flapping carpet slippers. If the butler wasn't quick about it, the President himself was likely to answer the White House doorbell which had been installed not long before. For this lack in her husband's "polish" of dress, manners, and speech, Mrs. Lincoln tried hard to compensate with her often-criticized elaborate receptions and expensive ball gowns.

For a while it was considered the democratic thing to invite the public to Presidential inaugural balls or levees, as they were called. Unhappily, shocking scenes occurred. After the popular hero, Andrew Jackson, was sworn into office in 1829, some 20,000 people stormed the White House. They rudely argued and jostled with each other to get at the bowls of rum punch, the fancy cakes, the ice cream. Windows, chairs, and priceless china were smashed. Worst of all was the spitting that resulted from all the tobacco chewing and snuff-sniffing.

How were the occupants of the White House itself to be treated? They were, after all, only temporary residents. The house belonged to the American people. Ought not citizens to be allowed to look over their own property whenever they chose? The poor occupants of the White House had little privacy. Not until 1864, when there were wartime threats against Lincoln's life, were guards posted to protect a President.

Evening fashion for ladies.

When President Lincoln was inaugurated again in 1865, Washington had changed since Abigail Adams had first seen it. But its streets had not changed enough. They were, according to the New York *Herald:*

> *. . . flooded and afloat with a vile yellow fluid, not thick enough to walk on nor thin enough to swim in. This yellow material added to the holiday appearance of the people, marking them with gay and festive spots from head to heel. All the backs were yellow with it, and all the horses, and all the little boys—all the world floundered about in it, and swore at it, and laughed at it.*

To Be a Child in Lincoln's Time

7

It meant many different things, of course, to be a child in Lincoln's time. It depended upon who the family was, where they lived and whether the time was 1800 or 1860. For ways of living changed rapidly during that half century.

This was especially true of home discipline. There were still chores to keep a boy or girl out of mischief. If you were a girl there was knitting, minding the baby, churning the butter, and learning housewifely skills. If you were a boy, there was milking the cow, laying a rail fence, and bringing in the firewood. You had some of these tasks even if you lived in a town or a small city. But as times changed, harsh discipline became less common. Parents no longer demanded instant, unquestioning obedience from their children. Instead, a visitor from abroad now complained of the "assumption, self-assertion, and conceit of American boys and girls." Another wrote that "baby citizens are allowed to run wild as the Snake Indians and do whatever they please."

Of course this was an exaggeration, but there had certainly been a revolution in the bringing up of children. The colonial child had been expected to be seen and not heard. Praise had been sparing. Now the Reverend Timothy Dwight wrote in his *Travels in New England and New York* that city children were being praised openly in a way that was likely to turn their heads—"You are a fine little fellow; you are a sweet little girl; my son, can't you speak one of your pieces before this good company?"

Abraham Lincoln was such an indulgent parent. His own boyhood had been one of all work and no play on the rough frontier. In his adult years children on the Western frontier were having the same kind of hard and trying childhood he himself had had. Many people marveled that the President was so lenient with his own sons. Willie and Tadd, for instance, liked nothing better than playing tricks on him. Sometimes they hid as he came down the street in Springfield, or later in Washington, and threw pebbles at his tall beaver hat, hoping to knock it off and watch the papers fly. Then they, too, flew. But their legs were never fast enough. Lincoln swept down on them with a few long strides, tucked a boy under each arm, and all three went laughing into the house for dinner, instead of to the woodshed for a whipping. To adult onlookers, even in a child-indulgent period, this was shocking.

Only rich children knew the joy of visiting a toy shop.

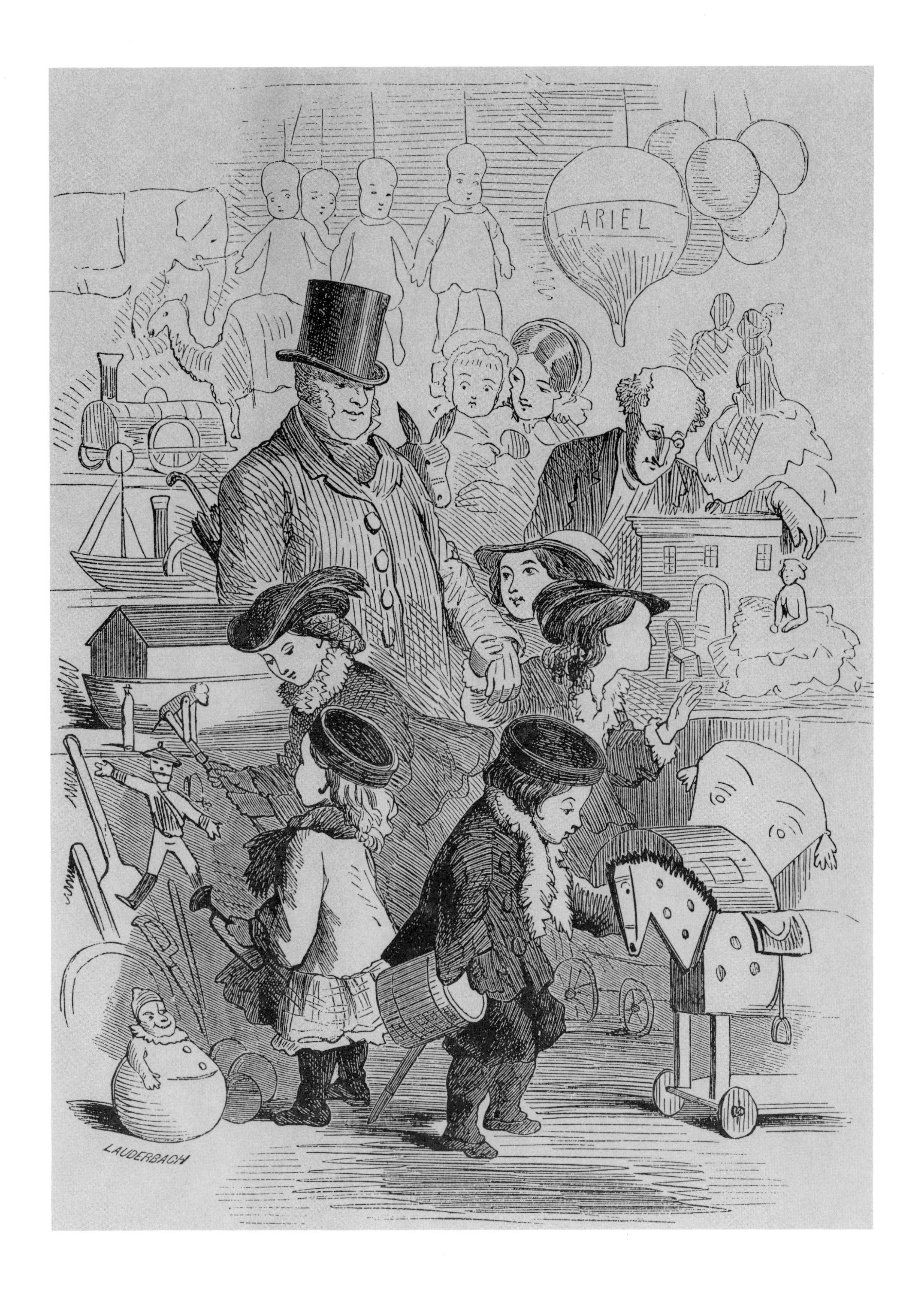
ARIEL
LAUDERBACH

Fashionable teenagers enjoying the first touch of winter. Below: A prim miss.

But America was growing, and possibilities for the boy with courage, nerve, and imagination were endless. Every boy might some day become President or become rich. Every girl might wake up to find herself the bride of such a man. Glorious possibilities like these were not for mild young people whose initiative had been blighted by discipline.

Faith in Flannel

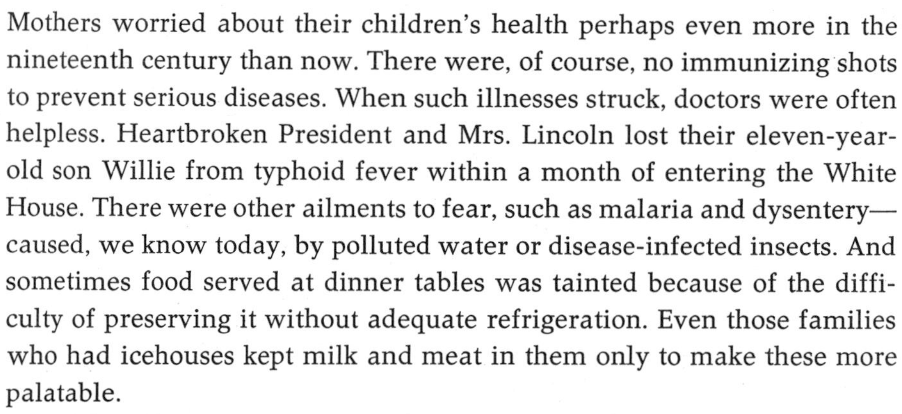

Mothers worried about their children's health perhaps even more in the nineteenth century than now. There were, of course, no immunizing shots to prevent serious diseases. When such illnesses struck, doctors were often helpless. Heartbroken President and Mrs. Lincoln lost their eleven-year-old son Willie from typhoid fever within a month of entering the White House. There were other ailments to fear, such as malaria and dysentery—caused, we know today, by polluted water or disease-infected insects. And sometimes food served at dinner tables was tainted because of the difficulty of preserving it without adequate refrigeration. Even those families who had icehouses kept milk and meat in them only to make these more palatable.

Mothers had some definite ideas of their own as to how to prevent their children from becoming ill. One stand-by was flannel worn next to the skin in all kinds of weather. An eleven-year-old boy who was visiting relatives in Georgia in the midsummer of 1830, when the temperature was probably in the nineties, wrote this desperate appeal home:

> *... tell dear mother that cousin Bet will not let me pull off my flannen, that she would if she was me take off everything but the flannen ...*

Baths, though taken far less often then than now, were another problem to boys and girls. There was a choice of washing in the frigid water from the back-porch pump or in the often scalding water of a large metal tub set in the kitchen before a roaring fire. Homemade lye soap burned sensitive skins almost unbearably. What a blessing it was to children when a mild castile soap began to be manufactured and was sold across the counters of the village store in mid-century.

From Flour Sack to Flounced Muslin

After the bath, pioneer children until late in the century wore coarse, scratchy, linsey-woolsey garments woven and sewn by their mothers and older sisters. Children of the slums and those who worked in the new factories dressed very simply. Boys wore short pants and a loose shirt made from a tow cloth such as that used for cornmeal or flour sacks; girls often wore a shift, which was sometimes no more than a flour sack with holes cut for head and arms. They often went barefoot for lack of shoes.

The richer or more socially ambitious the parents, the more elaborate the child's dress. The fashions for little girls mimicked those of their mothers, as fashions for little girls usually do. Their lawn or muslin dresses were flounced and ruffled; so were their petticoats and pantalettes. Boys wore plain, rather tightly fitted trousers down to their highly polished shoes and loose white shirts with long sleeves. Sometimes there was an open collar, often ruffled or pleated, and sometimes a black string tie.

Some mothers kept their little sons in dresses with ruffled collars until what we would think an embarrassingly advanced age. Sometimes the boys even wore curls to match.

The height of fashion for the very young.

Blab Schools

Whatever Americans may have disagreed about, there is one subject on which they have agreed perfectly from the beginning: schooling for every child. The Founding Fathers built first a church, then a schoolhouse. And *The Farmer's Almanac* advised: "The prudent farmer looks first to three things to prepare for winter: secure your cellars from frost; fasten loose clapboards and shingles; and secure a good schoolmaster."

But Americans have never agreed as to just how their schools should carry out this aim. The whole story of education in the United States has been one of experimenting, of searching for the ideal ways to teach and learn. Now we use "teaching machines" and television classes in an effort to make some areas of learning painless and even pleasurable. The nineteenth century would have been horrified at the thought of making a game out of learning. It believed that children should be deeply grateful for the blessing of an education and should work to acquire it. Sugarcoating the process was unthinkable. The very purpose of education was for them a moral one. The drudgery of rote learning was supposed to train a child's character to be disciplined, persevering, tough of fiber.

In the early 1800's, America's schools were still in a primitive state. Certainly the opportunity for every child to learn even the most elementary reading, writing, and "ciphering"—as arithmetic was called—was still only a hope. Those lucky enough to be able to pay for the "three R's" went to "blab schools," like those of their colonial forebears. Both the one-room "little red schoolhouse" and the fashionable Infant or Dame Schools of town and city were of this kind.

Abraham Lincoln was a blab school pupil. When he was five years old, little Abe walked with his sister Sarah the four miles from their family's Knob Creek cabin in Kentucky to the nearest schoolhouse. Here they endured every kind of physical discomfort. The schoolroom floor was of hardpacked clay; the puncheon or split log benches had no backs. The pot-bellied iron stove roasted those who sat near it, but left those in the far corners with chills and chilblains. During the winter months, water in the drinking pail was covered with a film of ice.

Young Abe attended this first school for only a few months. For the rest of his life he formed the words he read with his mouth, instead of reading them silently. At blab school he had been taught to study aloud.

Prank-playing boys force a stove to smoke by stuffing it with rags.

Children enjoy a singing lesson at an old Lutheran schoolhouse.

What a din, with every pupil intoning his lessons in a droning singsong! But this was the accepted way for the schoolmaster or mistress to be sure no boy or girl was daydreaming while the teacher taught the various grades gathered in the same room. Children of all ages, from four or five to as much as eighteen years, sat side by side throughout their entire school careers.

Wandering Schoolmasters

Schoolmasters were usually young men who carried their store of learning, sometimes meager, from settlement to settlement. There could be school only when there was a teacher. He was usually welcomed eagerly by all except a few half-grown rowdies. To these the new master sometimes had to prove himself with his fists before they would respect his brains. He was given room and board in the home of a pupil. Other parents paid him in furs, venison, hams, maple sugar, tobacco, or whatever else took the place of money in the neighborhood. No schools were free or supported by taxes in the early 1800's.

The itinerant teachers were a mixed lot. Most were young men who hoped somehow to make their fortunes in the newly opened West. Some had planned to become lawyers, ministers of the Gospel, or physicians, but had failed to make the grade. Instead, they had to peddle their small stock of learning to pupils in the one-room schoolhouses of the West and the Near-West, or perhaps in a district school in Eastern farm country.

Many were not happy in their work; perhaps that is why they so often used the birch rod when their authority or knowledge was questioned. Many of them obviously had little learning and less patience.

The Blue-backed Speller

A new scholar began by endlessly repeating the alphabet aloud. Next he mastered lists of syllables which introduced him to all the possible sounds in the English-American language. Usually he used Noah Webster's *American Spelling Book,* the famous "blue-backed speller," as everyone called it, and the most popular textbook ever written. By 1804, twenty years after it came out, over two million copies of this little book had been sold. By the mid-1800's, the count was close to seventy-five million. It was carried as a family treasure westward across America in countless covered wagons, along with the pewter teapot and roots of sage, mint, thyme, and rosemary from the New England garden that had been left behind. In a raw new country where books were few, most households had only two volumes: the Bible and Webster's speller, 119 pages long.

The author himself, carrying it in his saddlebags, peddled it up and down the Atlantic coastline for only seven cents a copy. Of this, the publisher took six cents and Webster received only one for himself. Lesson I, to be recited rhythmically, went:

Newsboys hawk their papers on city streets.

At night the newsboys struggle to get some schooling.

ba	*be*	*bi*	*bo*	*bu*	*by*
ca	*ce*	*ci*	*co*	*cu*	*cy*
da	*de*	*di*	*do*	*du*	*dy*

When he had learned twelve such lessons, a beginning pupil progressed to rows of spelling words. After mastering these, he read his first story, composed entirely of one-syllable words:

> *A good child will not lie, swear, nor steal. He will be good at home, and ask to read his book; when he gets up he will wash his hands and face clean; he will comb his hair, and make haste to school; he will not play by the way, as bad boys do.*

All stories in the *Speller* were highly moral. America, though less strict in beliefs and practice than it had been, was still part-Puritan. It approved of a schoolbook that included a story of a small boy who stole his neighbor's apples, because it showed beneath the text a woodcut of the neighbor brandishing a stout stick. It liked stories with titles like "Two Hasty and Inconsiderate Dogs," "Good Boy Versus Bad," "Peter the Miser; Harry the Glutton." It especially liked maxims at the end of a story such as: "Let your sins past put you in mind to mend," "When wine is in, wit is out," and "A good cow may have a bad calf."

Almost stifled by clothing, girls spend a day at the seashore playing cat's cradle.

W H

Lessons did not remain easy. Soon the young scholar, still in what we would call a primary grade, was learning to spell such words as collateral, manifesto, panegyric, misanthrophy, malefactor, and polytheism. With reading, spelling, and a bit of "ciphering" as far as the "Rule of 3" (that is, the three-times table) went lessons in writing. Most people who learned to write at all wished to "write a good hand" as a matter of pride. Abe Lincoln practiced his writing with a piece of charcoal on a wooden fire shovel. He then scraped off the letters and began again.

Love of long words led to the spelling bee, which became almost a national sport. On Saturday nights, spectators for miles around would jam the little red schoolhouse to cheer their favorite speller. The audience clapped, stamped, and shouted. It didn't matter that the champion speller might not know what such a winning word as "antidisestablishmentarianism" meant. The great thing was that he could spell such a "jawbreaker."

When eleven years old, Abe attended his last school, at Pigeon Creek, Indiana. The session lasted only a few months, for school "kept" for only a short part of each year, usually the dead of winter. In pioneer and farm country, crops needed planting, tending, harvesting, and these required the help of every member of a family. Education could wait; ripening wheat could not.

Little men and women.

McGuffey's Readers

Another writer of schoolbooks as important as Noah Webster's was William Holmes McGuffey. By the age of thirteen this bright boy was already teaching in the country schools of the Ohio Territory. Soon he, too, decided that America needed its own textbooks, not warmed-over English ones. His series of *Eclectic Readers* ("eclectic" meant "a selecting or sorting out") began to appear in 1836.

McGuffey, like most editors and teachers of the time, believed that education should train character. So he selected stories, poems and exercises that had a pious tinge. The moral was almost always clear and conspicuous. But it was also sometimes a worldly moral, preaching the doctrine that if you were good, you would be rewarded in this world—sometimes with fame, sometimes with gold. It even went so far as to say that if you did a good deed, such as helping an old man cross the street, he might remember you in his will. New Englanders were known not only for being puritanical but also for being shrewd.

Year after year, millions of Americans read these books in school. They read such poems as "The Boy Stood on the Burning Deck," "The Old Oaken Bucket," "Meddlesome Mattie," and Longfellow's "Psalm of Life," as well as passages from the Bible and scenes from Shakespeare. They studied stories called "Do Not Meddle," "The Gentle Hand," "Respect for the Sabbath Rewarded," and a little sermon entitled "Control Your Temper." They read John Greenleaf Whittier's "The Fish I Never Caught"

A master hurries his two young chimney sweeps along a fashionable city street.

and Nathaniel Hawthorne's nostalgic "The Town Pump." Some were literature of genuine and lasting value; others were examples of the sentimental kind of writing that was popular at the time. Because they appeared in a *McGuffey Reader,* such poems as the following became a part of America's heritage: "Mary Had a Little Lamb," "Twinkle, Twinkle, Little Star," and "If at First You Don't Succeed, Try, Try Again!" They were a kind of national mental porridge.

Even books intended to be bought as gifts for children and read for pleasure were mostly still highly moral. Not until the early 1800's had there been such a thing as a child's book. The first ones were written and printed by Samuel Goodrich of Ridgefield, a Connecticut printer and engraver who composed and illustrated with woodcuts some 170 "toy" books, as he called them. "Toy" they were: each book only two by four inches in size, their pages sewn together by hand and the pictures tinted by hand with watercolors. Here is a sample verse from a book by Peter Parley, as the author called himself:

> *Those who love to loiter and play,*
> *And good advice will throw away;*
> *They must without a supper go,*
> *And lose their share of plum-cakes, too.*

Training for Proper Young Ladies

By "education for all children," Americans meant that girls, too, should learn the three R's. Dame Schools were for boys and girls, but the sexes were separated by an aisle. Teachers were gentlewomen, usually widowed, poor, and proud—and often not much better educated than the children they taught. After finishing the Dame School, boys and girls would never again attend school together. The boys who stayed in school studied subjects thought fit to prepare them for the man's world of business and the professions. A girl slipped quietly back into the position of a loving daughter, helping her mother churn and bake and care for the baby, embroidering a sampler in her spare time. When we see the fine stitching of an old sampler still hanging on a parlor wall, we tend to think, "Imagine her having to spend so many hours indoors, sewing those pious verses in such tiny stitches." We forget that this was the way a girl learned her letters and numbers, as well as how to spell and print her name.

A cornshucking machine and a churn made children's chores lighter.

Finishing Schools for Young Ladies taught what it was believed every young girl should know if she was to become an accomplished and charming young lady; later a gracious wife and hostess. This meant studying conversational French, piano or singing lessons, drawing, embroidery, and "literature"—including only those novels and poetry thought proper for a young lady's eyes. The Reverend Timothy Dwight, President of Yale from 1795 to 1817, was concerned about the pap with which girl's minds were being fed. He wrote:

> *The reading of girls is regularly lighter than that of boys. When the standard of reading for boys is set too low, that for girls will be proportionately lowered . . . When the utmost labour of boys is bounded by history, biography, and the pamphlets of the day: girls sink down to song, novels, and plays.*

By their censored, watered-down education, young girls were given wholly false and romantic ideas about life. The heroes of whom they read were dream men living in the mansions of the novelist's imagination. How disappointed such a girl would be when she discovered that not every young man, once married, is "as handsome, as dignified, as brave, as generous, as affectionate, as faithful, and as accomplished" as her novel-reading had led her to believe.

That girls needed an education of sorts everyone agreed. But of what kind? Unfortunately, there were still people who could, as late as 1864, assert:

> *The race of strong, hardy, cheerful girls—the girls that could wash, iron, brew, bake, tackle a horse and drive him, no less than braid straw, embroider, draw, paint, and read innumerable books—this race of women, pride of olden time, is daily lessening; and in their stead come the fragile, languid girls of a modern age, drilled in book learning, ignorant of common things.*

There *were,* however, schools which aimed at turning out well-rounded girls. In 1847, Emily Dickinson, who later became one of America's finest poets, spent a year at Mount Holyoke Seminary, which was later to become the nation's first woman's college. A letter written to her friend Abiah, describes a typical day at the seminary:

> *At 6 o'clock, we all rise. We breakfast at 7. Our study hours begin at 8. At 9 we all meet in Seminary Hall for devotions. At 10-1/4 I recite a review of Ancient History . . . At 11 I recite a lesson in "Pope's Essay on Man." . . . At 12 I practise Calisthenics and at 12-1/4 read until dinner which is 12-1/2. After dinner from 1-1/2 until 2 I sing in Seminary Hall. From 2-1/4 I go to Section, where we give in our accounts for the day, including Absence—Tardiness—Communications—Breaking Silent Study Hours—Receiving Company in our rooms and ten thousand other things which I will not take time or place to mention. At 4-1/4 we go to Seminary Hall and receive advice from Miss Lyon in the form of a lecture. We have supper at 6 and silent study hours from then until the retiring bell, which rings at 8-1/4 . . .*

Nothing to do but turn the handle.

Here was a no-nonsense school. The severe and brilliant Miss Mary Lyon, who was its head, believed that young ladies should learn to work with their hands as well as their heads. In addition to the routine described above, Emily Dickinson had to lay out knives for the meals at night and noon, and wash and wipe them in the evening. Clearly the Puritan values of industry, careful use of time, and self-discipline had not vanished.

The First Free Schools

Most boys and girls attended school only just long enough to learn to read and write—for about three years. For the few boys who meant to become ministers, doctors or lawyers, fine academies or private schools were established. These prepared serious young scholars for college. In them

With calliope playing and flags flying, the circus parades through a covered bridge on its way to the waiting village.

the course of study was severe. It centered on the Greek and Roman classics, taught in their original languages, and included philosophy, logic, religion, mathematics, and declamation (or public speaking).

But a thin crust of educated men on the surface of the plain bread of American society was not enough. Horace Mann, a New England educator with advanced ideas about schools and teaching methods, presented a powerful argument for free education when he wrote in 1848, "Education . . . is the great equalizer of men . . . It does better than to disarm the poor of their hostility toward the rich; it prevents being poor." Here *was* a new idea. Educations' purpose might go beyond teaching children how to be good; it could also show them how to grow rich! From this time on, the drive for educating every child at public expense grew stronger year by year throughout the country. New England was the pace-setter: the first public high school to open its doors to all qualified boys was the Boston Latin School in 1821.

A Time for Fun

"The circus is coming! The circus is coming!" What words could have been more exciting on a fine summer morning than these? Overnight,

while the children slept, someone had posted great red, yellow, and black signs on every tree trunk, covered bridge, and board fence in town. They screamed the news:

> *CIRCUS! The WORLD'S BIGGEST FAT LADY! Six enormous ELEPHANTS from DISTANT INDIA! WILD ANIMALS galore! Bareback RIDERS from the WILD WEST! Mr. NELLIS, the ARMLESS WONDER! MR. PIERCE in a DEN OF LIONS!*

It was quite enough to turn a village boy's head from watering the cows or running errands for his mother. For two weeks or so, such a boy wasn't much use to anybody. But, come CIRCUS DAY, he was up betimes—and off to the circus grounds.

Early in the nineteenth century the circus had begun to evolve from the traveling wild animal show into something more complex. Now it also meant: "Tumbling Arabs"; a lion tamer; a bareback "Apollo on Horseback"; a circus parade, with its bandwagon, calliope, and the "World's Largest Fat Lady" riding in a gorgeous open red and gold carryall drawn by six white horses.

What did country boys and girls do with their spare time on ordinary days? Many of the same things that children do today—in winter, sledding and ice skating, and in summer, swimming in the "old swimming hole" and poling homemade rafts on lake and river. They fished for brook and lake trout. They hunted rabbit and squirrel, 'possum and woodchuck. Trapping and hunting were sports with a practical purpose, but sport just the same. In winter, Northern boys fished through holes in the ice on a lake, and hunting was easier, for rabbits and bobcats left their tracks in the snow.

Wilderness children often combined their play with a purpose, as in berry picking and nutting. They had one delight all their own: baby animals of the forest to tame for pets. Racoon and otter, squirrel, fawn, even bear cub took readily to the ways of men and often made delightful pets. These made up in part for a child's not having any next-door friends. Some wilderness children made flutter wheels in a nearby brook. "Creeper" or grapevine swings hung ready for the using on the edge of the forest. Older brothers and sisters carved wooden dolls and horses as "play pretties" for the baby. A busy mother sometimes stole time from her daylong work to dress a corncob doll for a little daughter.

City children rolled beer barrel hoops in the park, and in winter skated on the pond. After 1854, a boy might own a handsome pair of wooden ice skates with shining metal runners. They played a form of Prisoner's Base or Pirate Catch, Blind Man's Bluff, and Go Hide. There were no bicycles, no chemistry sets, no space toys. Younger children played store, "livery stable" and "stagecoach." Little girls copied their mothers at miniature housekeeping. For the child whose papa could afford it, there might be a rocking horse or a wicker cart to be pulled by a large dog or pony.

An adventurous boy tries a walk on stilts.

Young imaginations were given good exercise, for there were few toys except homemade ones. If an uncle had a way with a piece of soft wood and a jackknife, a boy was lucky. Then the boy might own a sailboat, rigged out with bits of cloth for sails. He might have a little Noah's Ark filled with tiny animals, two of every kind, and perhaps a set of wooden blocks, a whistle, or even a bow and some arrows. If the child were a girl, the uncle might whittle a wooden doll fitted with jointed arms and legs, to be dressed by an older sister. And perhaps there would even be a doll-house with furniture.

Few toys were manufactured in America until mid-century. Most were imported from France, Germany, and Switzerland, where whole villages had been making toys for generations. French dolls were beautiful. They often had wigs of real hair and were dressed in the height of fashion. Also from abroad came wooden replicas of the Buckingham Palace guard, knights on horseback, boards on which to play peg and marble games, drums, and rocking horses with real manes and green glass eyes. There were even intricate toys with moving parts and music boxes with a dancing clown or acrobat on top—all fitted with Swiss clockworks inside.

But these were very expensive. In America no one thought of starting a toy factory until 1840, when a tin factory in Meriden, Connecticut, began using up scraps by making toys from them. Other factories in Philadelphia and New York followed their example. Soon it was possible to buy cheap

In imitation of the real thing, the horse bus cuts a pretty figure. At right: Toy monkey on a stick.

replicas of animals, wagons, penny banks, toy dishes and pails. Soon after 1833 a rubber factory began making balloons.

By midcentury, as new inventions amazed the adult world, toy models of these soon appeared for sale in city shops with a few even finding their way to the Yankee pedlar's wagon: wooden trains, prairie schooners, a tiny tin steamboat, or a model fire engine with a bell. In the Shelburne Museum in Vermont there is even a little tin merry-go-round that still goes round and round when pushed gently.

Edward Everett Hale, born in Boston in 1822 and later a clergyman, was encouraged to make his own playthings. He and his brother set up a press of their own, using cast-off type from their father's newspaper office, and printed little booklets, three or four inches square. In one Edward published a poem he had written about the wonders of the new steam transportation. One stanza proclaimed:

First then, we find, that by steam-engine's power,
We now can move full eighteen miles an hour;
And what ten years ago untrue would seem,
Is now accomplished perfectly by steam.

From Boston Pulpit to Wilderness Camp Meeting

8

Although the stern Puritan spirit was just beginning to fade in the early 1800's, it was far from dead. Josiah Quincy wrote of his six boyhood years at Andover Academy, "We had come to Andover to get religion"—not *learning,* but *religion.* At the Sunday morning service which the young scholars had to attend, there was no heating even in the dead of winter, and it was so cold that the water in the baptismal font froze. At the other extreme, on the hottest day of summer, the master said, as he dismissed the boys, "There will now be a prayer meeting: those who wish to lie down in everlasting burning may go; the rest will stay." Only two boys, Josiah Quincy one of them, had the audacity to walk out.

From 1820 to 1830 there were distinct signs that Puritan severity was softening. Why had God created things of beauty, some men were asking, if He had meant these to be ignored? Was it not possible that some of the spirit of the Creator was reflected in good qualities found in men? If so, the possibilities for human betterment were boundless. Such writers as Emerson, Longfellow, and Walt Whitman were inspired by this optimistic view of man's and America's future. The new attitude spread so quickly that by mid-century the rest of the world pictured the typical American as hopeful, dauntless, and filled with high dreams.

However, religion itself remained a strong influence in American life. The Sabbath was still a dismal day. No games were allowed, not even for little children, and no visiting or reading, except of the Bible or religious books. A Frenchman wrote: "Nothing is, therefore, more melancholy than the seventh day in this country; after such a Sunday, the labor of Monday is a delightful pastime." But God was remembered not only on Sunday. In the 1840's, someone has estimated, three-fourths of the reading material circulating in America consisted of religious tracts, journals, and newspapers.

In variety of religions, America had, of course, come a long way since the seventeenth century, when the very settlers who had once sought religious freedom had denied it to Quaker, Jew, and Roman Catholic. Every city could now boast a great variety of churches. In 1830, Boston had forty-three; New York and Philadelphia more than a hundred each. There were Protestant and Roman Catholic churches, Jewish synagogues, and many mushrooming small sects—some destined to wither, others to grow.

Wilderness Religion—the Circuit Rider

Despite the rain, Anabaptists in Philadelphia carry on with a baptismal immersion.

In the back country and the wilderness, life was very different. Here there were often no organized churches at all. Or, if there was a crude church, there was probably no resident preacher. To fill this gap, a new kind of preacher sprang up—the "circuit rider." These were dedicated men who had "heard the call" to preach to their fellows. Most of them had no special training for their calling. But many possessed moral courage, intense conviction, a magnetic personality, a hypnotic if sometimes rude eloquence, and stamina. These were qualities beloved by the frontiersman. To such a preacher's message the pioneer and his family would listen, spellbound.

The gestures of the itinerant preacher were often highly dramatic and unrestrained. Abe Lincoln expressed his preference thus: "The fact is I don't like to hear cut-and-dried sermons. When I hear a man preach, I like to see him act as if he were fighting bees." Most of his backwoods neighbors would have agreed with him. The Rev. Peter Cartwright was this kind of man of God. In his *Autobiography* he wrote:

Horses splash their way through the shallows of a river to bring passengers to camp meeting. Right: Arrived at last, the people pray in a tent.

A . . . preacher in those days, when he felt that God had called him to preach, instead of hunting up a college or Biblical institute, hunted up a hardy pony or horse . . . and with his library always at hand, namely, Bible, Hymn Book, and Discipline, he started . . . Often he slept in dirty cabins, on earthen floors, before the fire; ate roastingears for bread, drank buttermilk for coffee, or sage tea for imperial; took, with a hearty zest, deer or bear meat, or wild turkey, for breakfast, dinner, and supper, if he could get it. His text was alway ready, "Behold the Lamb of God," etc. This was old-fashioned . . . preacher fare and fortune.

Camp Meeting

So the circuit preacher took to the rough roads and trails, usually on horseback. Upon his arrival in a thinly populated district, the log church house, if there happened to be one, was joyfully opened. The news spread, and "meeting" was held for days and nights at a time. If a building was lacking, an open-air "camp meeting" was called. From miles roundabout the people gathered at the camp ground, bringing their children with them. Some came with tents: others built temporary lean-tos of tree branches and brush. All brought cooking pots and food. They hacked out rough benches and a speaker's platform from logs. At night they built a bonfire.

Camp meeting was religion, excitement, entertainment, comfort, sociability all rolled into one. The lonely people of the back country were hungry to renew their awareness of a tie with the church "back home."

Denominational differences were usually forgotten for the time being, since it was agreed that almost any preacher must be on the side of the angels. So he was given a respectful ear as he preached that his listeners must confess their sins, stop drinking, gambling, loafing, and fighting. Women must cease all backbiting, gossip, and sloth. Hell, an uncomfortably hot place in which to spend eternity, was the reward promised to those whose hearts remained hard and cold to the "message."

A contagious excitement was generated at these camp meetings. Hymns, their pitch set by tuning fork, harmonica, or fiddle, were sung by the hour. Secular dancing was frowned upon, and whole sermons were preached to prove that King David could not have meant it when he said in the Book of Ecclesiastes, "There is a time to dance." Yet, under the influence of the popular jig tunes to which many hymns were set, singers joined each other in the aisles and "marched" in a kind of writhing joy that certainly bordered on the dance. They chanted:

I am bound for the Kingdom!
Will you go to Glory with me?
O *Hallelujah!* O *Halle, Hallelujah!*
I am bound for the Kingdom!

With scores of lamps scattered among the trees, more than a thousand people gather at a camp meeting to hear a preacher's exhortations.

Left: Quakers outside their Meeting House on Arch Street, Philadelphia. Right: First time at church!

Prayer followed prayer. Emotions reached such a pitch that worshipers shouted, clapped their hands, rolled on the ground, and "got religion." Scoffers were prayed over and warned grimly of hell fire. When camp meeting was over, life went back to its harsh and dull routine. Yet a kind of glow remained in the heart. The circuit rider's visit had satisfied many needs of these lonely, forest-imprisoned, hard-working people.

When enough members had gathered in a district to support a church, they built a crude house of worship and hired a preacher to live among them. They built him a cabin like their own and paid his salary in hides and corn, in wool, lumber, molasses, even whisky. From this point on, the settlement church followed the pattern of the early churches of the eastern seaboard.

From Handicraft to Machine

9

It is a cause for wonder that America was a nation built mostly by hand, with no machine for servant. Horsepower and waterpower played a part, but it was human brawn, ingenuity and nimble fingers that did the initial work: two hundred years of felling giant trees with an ax, of building houses, of clearing and tilling fields with hand tools and horse-drawn implements, of making wooden pegs for nails; of cooking food in a fireplace, of shearing sheep, carding wool, spinning thread, weaving cloth, and finally sewing the shirt—all painfully by hand-operated shears, carder, spinning wheel, loom and needle.

For many years each household in raw colonial America was almost completely self-sustaining. A homesteader was his own carpenter, cabinetmaker, cobbler, barber, miller, as well as farmer and hunter. His lady was seamstress, tailor, dairymaid, soap and candlemaker, dyer, mixer of herb remedies, as well as housewife and mother. Gradually a few men in each settlement began to specialize in the work they did best. Carpenters, millers, silver and tinsmiths, cobblers, glass blowers, candlemakers set up shops. But the work was still done by hand or with crude hand-operated machines, slowly and laboriously. Sometimes it was done beautifully by such gifted artisans as Duncan Phyfe, whose handsome handcrafted chairs and tables are now the pride of our museums, and the models for our furniture factories. These specialists set up a system of apprentices to whom they taught their particular skills.

But even after traditional ways of doing work had been established, men, particularly in New England, continued to experiment with new and easier ways of doing old tasks. Thus was born the machine, and, with the machine, a whole new life for Americans.

The Miraculous Cotton Gin

Eli Whitney's cotton gin—"gin" was an abbreviation of "engine"—ushered in this new life. Since the days of ancient Egypt, it had taken a long day's labor for one man to pick seeds from a single pound of cotton. Now, even with the unperfected gin, one man could do in a day the work of fifty. Its invention made cotton the king of America's field products.

The circular saws of Whitney's gin were at first hand-turned within a cylinder. The saws pulled the cotton fibers, but not the seeds, into the cage.

By 1850 hundreds of thousands of girls were employed in factories of all kinds.

Soon steam power was applied. By the early 1800's, our exports of raw cotton to other countries had multiplied by thirty times. Cotton-picking slaves were much in demand all over the Deep South as more and more plantation owners planted every possible acre in cotton. Indirectly the cotton gin was one of the causes of the Civil War. For with its invention countless more slaves were needed; therefore, the slave trade and the slave population of the cotton-planting states burgeoned.

England was especially eager for America's cotton. It already had the "Spinning Jenny" and the power loom. These were hungry for cotton to spin into thread, then weave into cloth. Before long, machines like these were set up in New England and in those southern states where cotton was grown. Priced at a few cents a yard, fat bolts of calico, dimity, and muslin found their way to the counters of city and country stores. Others were carried by the Yankee peddler to the most out-of-the-way farm. The cloth was sprigged with roses or forget-me-nots; it was checked and flecked with color that made it alluring to a color-hungry people. It was cheap. Most important of all, in every home to which it found its way, cotton yard goods released women and girls from their long enslavement to spinning wheel and loom.

The Passing of the Spinning Wheel

Until the 19th century, not only clothing but bedding, too, had been woven on hand looms. The fortunate few who could afford sheets did this irksome work themselves or had it done by weaver or slave. For centuries the most precious of a family's possessions had been its bedding. Now cotton mills began weaving sheets, then towels, curtains, and tablecloths for what seemed a small price.

A young Bostonian who visited England at the beginning of the nineteenth century was impressed by the textile factories there. In 1812 he built a similar factory on the bank of the Merrimack River in Massachusetts, but he improved upon the British loom by perfecting a machine powered by water instead of by hand. Soon the hum of water-driven looms in Francis Cabot Lowell's mill was louder in the land than the hum of the good wife's fireside treadle. Its citizens named their city "Lowell" in his honor.

This revolution in making cotton cloth happened early in the century. As the years went by, other fibers, too, were woven by machine in the

To make these hoop skirts more than 25,000 feet of whalebone and a ton of steel were used daily.

A Singer sewing machine of 1854.

new factories. Wool was made into fine broadcloth. Until he was a young lawyer in Springfield, Abraham Lincoln had worn only coarse homespun crudely sewn into ill-fitting suits. In 1834, newly elected to the Illinois state legislature, he bought his first black broadcloth, factory woven, for a fine new suit.

Silk mills were also set up; these, too, mainly in New England. Requiring water power, they were always built on the banks of swift streams. Until now the splendid silks—taffetas, satins, damasks—for the draperies and upholstery of well-to-do town houses had been woven abroad, chiefly in France. So had materials for the gowns of ladies of fashion. Now it was possible for Dolly Madison, Mrs. John Quincy Adams, and Mary Todd Lincoln to have their ball gowns made from lengths of silk spun and woven in Manchester, Connecticut.

Seamstresses and Sewing Machines

Many young girls fresh from the country or just off the boat from Ireland or Germany found employment as seamstresses. It was a day when every lady of fashion had her elaborate gowns handmade for her. Sewing for a modiste was a thoroughly respectable way for a young woman with little education and no money to support herself. Her working day was fourteen hours long, her pay shockingly low. Many wives of poor men also sewed to help with their family's support. They took "piecework" home with them. There, in the cold of their drab slum flats they plied needles with half-frozen fingers, while keeping an eye on the children.

Then in 1845, a Boston watchmaker apprentice named Elias Howe invented a vastly improved sewing machine. Instead of the laborious hand stitching that had been woman's age-old task, here was a machine which could make 250 stitches in one minute! Of course, some women continued to take pride in their hand stitching. But that was very different from being compelled to sew in the old way. Before long the lives of women were completely changed. Released from hemming the family's sheets and sewing their brothers shirts, more and more girls (whose fathers could afford the tuition) now attended the young ladies' seminaries springing up throughout the East and South. Some people even began to complain that the art of sewing would at this rate soon become extinct. Eventually the women of Boston succeeded in having sewing made a required course for girls in the new public schools of that city.

On the other hand, those girls who had to earn their keep found respectable jobs in factories. Now they sat in long rows manning the new power-driven machines, turning out sheets, petticoats, towels, and tablecloths—all for an America eager to buy articles "ready-made."

After a stagecoach journey through Massachusetts in 1838, Nathaniel Hawthorne described his first view of the new factories:

> *Along our road we passed villages, and often factories, the machinery whirring, and girls looking out of the windows at the stage, with heads averted from their tasks, but still busy. These factories have two, three, or more boarding houses near them, two stories high, and of double length—often with bean-vines running up round the doors, and with altogether a domestic look. There are several factories in different parts of North Adams, along the banks of a stream—a wild, highland rivulet, which, however, does a vast work of a civilized nature.*

A deep-crowned, wide-brimmed black felt hat called a William Penn.

A Factory for Every Need

The making of hats and shoes, of stockings and gloves, of thread and buttons all followed the same pattern. For years, bonnet straw braiding was a home industry in a number of New England towns. Village girls worked eagerly, their pay ranging from 2½ cents a yard to 4 cents for especially fine work. In 1859 a government patent was given for a "silk and straw weaving machine." Then the village lasses, who had so enjoyed their communal work around a single table with much chatter and laughter, were forced to find work in a large, noisy bonnet factory.

The mark of a nineteenth-century gentleman was his tall beaver hat—the kind in which Abraham Lincoln kept his important mail and papers. Into the making of these, fur-trappers poured their harvest of beaver pelts, and hatter apprentices sat at their benches for endless hours every working day. In 1823, a hat factory at Danbury, Connecticut, was turning out only two hats a day, with a demand many times greater than it could supply. In 1847, thanks to new steam-driven machines, 100,000 beaver hats poured onto the market from this one factory.

Now many more men could afford this symbol of gentlemanly status. Nathaniel Hawthorne found young apprentices and clerks wearing beaver hats on a Sunday afternoon in Boston to impress their young lady friends. "Sunday gentlemen," he called them. In the 1840's, the tall silk hat became the fashion. The demand for beaver furs fell off drastically. But the same machines whirred away, now turning out silk hats for gentlemen.

The story of clocks is equally fascinating. Ever since colonial days it had been possible to buy individually constructed wooden clockworks. This was a standard item in the Yankee peddler's wagon. Then, for another $20 or so, one had a cabinetmaker build a case for the mechanism. In 1800, Eli Terry of Plymouth Hollow, Connecticut, invented crude, water-driven tools that could manufacture ten to twenty clocks at a time. He soon found himself operating the first clock factory in America. His friends, Seth Thomas and Silas Hoadley, went into the business with him. By 1813, and with twenty hands to help, they were making 4000 clocks a year and selling them for $4 each. These clocks had wooden movements and cases of cherry, maple, and pine. Even this "breath-taking speed" of manufacture was not enough. Chauncey Jerome of near-by Bristol, Connecticut, began making clocks with works stamped out of sheet brass. Soon his workers were making 100,000 clocks a year. By 1847, more clocks were made in Connecticut than elsewhere in the world.

A black beaver with a stovepipe crown, 1865. Below: A beige felt bowler of 1870.

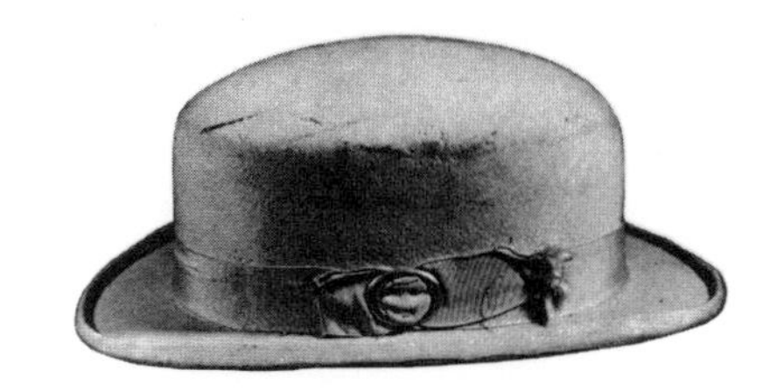

During these same years, the Associated Spring Company in Bristol, Connecticut, began by making clock works, but then found it more profitable to change to hoop skirts. Called "crinolines," these had flexible steel frames that held ladies' skirts in the huge bell shape approved by fashion.

Even as tiny an item as the button has a story. In 1802, two brothers, Levi and Abel Porter, wishing to set up a button factory, tried to buy brass from England, but were refused. So the ingenious fellows made their own brass from the metal of worn-out kettles mixed with zinc. Because Great Britain feared American competition, it forbade English brass workers to leave the country. But in 1812, the American Brass Company smuggled a number of skilled men out of England by hiding them in hogsheads and slipping them on board Yankee clipper ships. By 1847, there were six brass and copper foundries and rolling mills in Waterbury, Connecticut. In this one place there were also ten metal factories turning out thousands of shiny buttons in all kinds of designs and shapes—enough to supply Yankee peddlers and village stores all over America.

Oddly enough, America's production of iron and steel did not keep up with its development of other metal industries. There were large deposits of iron in the mountains around Pittsburgh, but the method of smelting ore was inferior. Besides, it was easier and cheaper for factory owners on the Eastern seaboard to import pig iron, steel, and coal from England than to transport it overland from western Pennsylvania.

Trains were to supply the answer here. They would make it possible to transport heavy goods of every kind from one end of the vast new country to the other. They would turn the Civil War into a new kind of conflict in which soldiers and supplies could be shifted faster than ever before. It became the prime objective of every commander to destroy the rail lines of the enemy.

More to Buy—and Cheaper

Over and over the story of Yankee ingenuity was repeated. Each invention meant new factory jobs, fewer hand chores, and cheaper products for sale both at home and abroad. There was silverware, for instance. The Rogers Brothers of Connecticut in 1842 developed a process whereby teapots and flatware of an alloy could be dipped in silver. They called their product "silver plate." At last it was possible for a housewife of moderate means to set her table with beautiful knives, forks, and spoons that looked like the solid silver that graced the tables of the very rich.

Glass blowers, too, created new and quicker ways of making both useful and pretty objects of glass. Since colonial days craftsmen had used the delicate process of blowing upon a molten mass of sand, potash, and lime through a metal tube, while deftly shaping it into a rough window pane or a crude glass bowl, pitcher, or goblet. About 1825, American glassmakers learned to press glass objects mechanically. Soon even a poor man could own a pressed glass whale oil lamp, saucers for his tea, and a paperweight (with a red rose magically imprisoned inside it) for his desk. Designs on pressed glass became more and more fanciful: eagles, clipper ships, sprays of wheat, hearts and arrows, and even the Bunker Hill Monument. The most beautiful glass of the nineteenth century was made at the Boston Sandwich Glass Company on Cape Cod, beginning in 1825. Its rich blues, amethyst, ruby, and topaz colors have never been matched. Sandwich glass is even today eagerly sought by private collectors and art museums.

Scenes of Indian battles, naval engagements and stagecoach holdups were engraved on the cylinders of almost all Colt revolvers.

Ever since colonial days little girls had spent endless hours braiding the rags of worn-out clothing for their mothers to stitch into rugs. Only the rich had been able to buy hand-woven carpets from Belgium and Persia. And only the home of a hunter could boast a bear or buffalo skin for its floor. In 1825, a power carpet loom was invented. Soon even the modest home could afford a factory-made carpet.

By 1840, it was also possible to buy factory-made soap—even special shaving soap. This meant no more leaching of fireplace ashes, no more

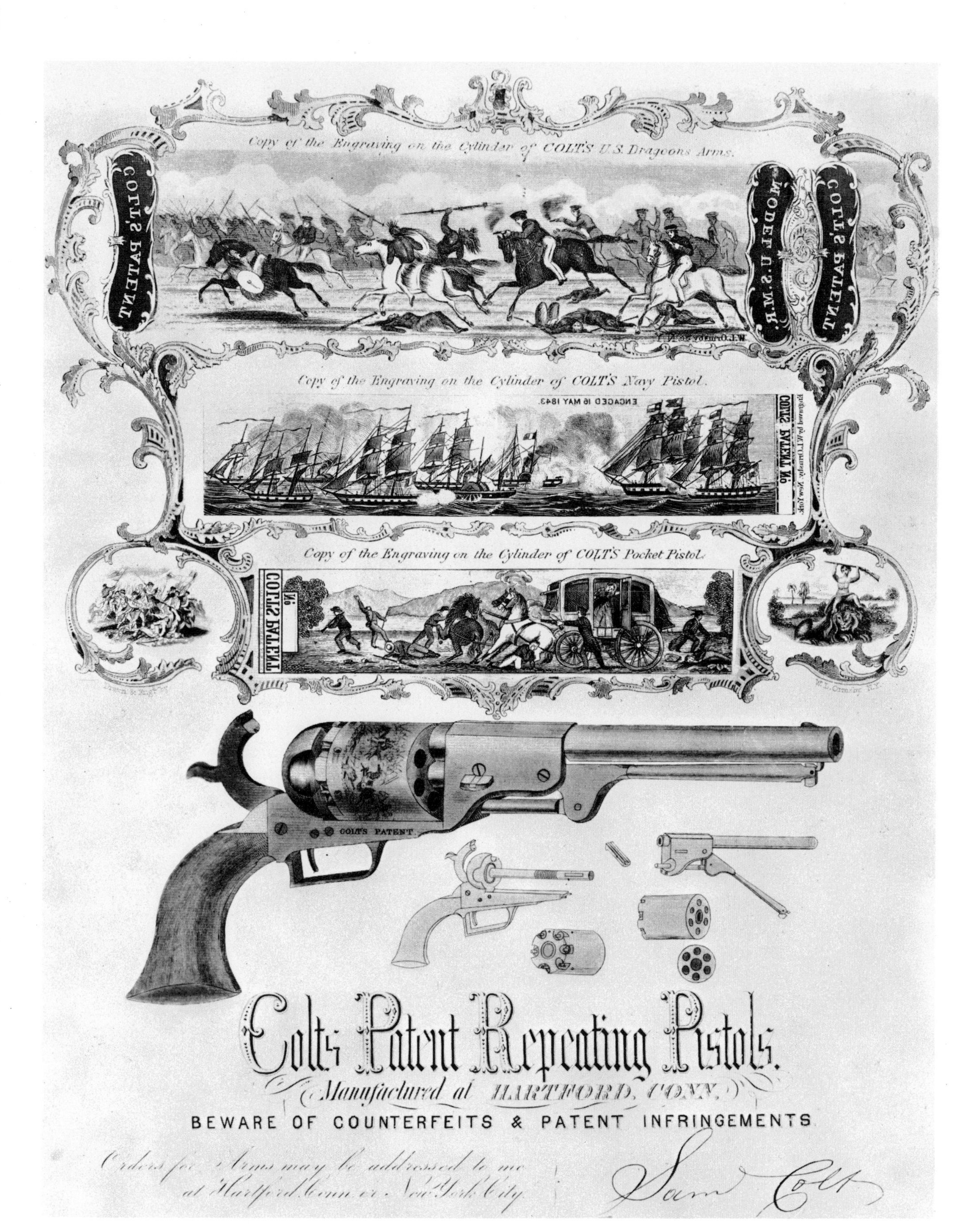
Copy of the Engraving on the Cylinder of COLT'S U.S. Dragoons Arms.
Copy of the Engraving on the Cylinder of COLT'S Navy Pistol.
Copy of the Engraving on the Cylinder of COLT'S Pocket Pistol.
COLT'S PATENT
Colts Patent Repeating Pistols.
Manufactured at HARTFORD, CONN.
BEWARE OF COUNTERFEITS & PATENT INFRINGEMENTS
Orders for Arms may be addressed to me
at Hartford Conn. or New York City.
Sam Colt

The testing of McCormick's miraculous reaper caused great excitement.

hours of stirring the evil-smelling backyard pot of hog fat and lye. It also meant no more delicate skins inflamed from the Saturday night bath with harsh homemade soap. Until now, only ladies with servants or slaves had been spared the chore of soapmaking. For years Mary Todd Lincoln had made all the soap for her family. What rejoicing there must have been among women when they could buy bars of pleasant-smelling, ready-made soap for a few pennies at the village store.

Brand-new Products

Some inventions produced brand-new products. One of these was the discovery in 1833 of the vulcanization of rubber. For years, clipper ships had been bringing this strange, sticky stuff as a curiosity from South America. Not until Charles Goodyear of Naugatuck, Connecticut, accidentally spilled some India rubber, as it was called, onto the coals of his kitchen fire did anyone learn that it could be made to serve many practical uses. Vulcanized rubber was flexible; when stretched, it would spring back to its original shape. And it was waterproof. By 1847, the Goodyear Rubber Company was manufacturing the world's first rubber gloves. Before long, rubber balls and balloons were being made. It was years before anyone thought of putting rubber tires on vehicles to make travel more comfortable.

Another invention which was to change the course of all future wars was the perfecting, by twenty-two-year-old Samuel Colt in 1836, of a breech-loading firearm with a revolving chamber. First he devised the pistol, then a shotgun and rifle. Within a month after patenting his inventions, the young man opened a factory for their manufacture. Within five years the United States government gave him a contract for a large order of the new weapons. By 1846, our country's victory in the Mexican War was credited to the superiority of our new weapons. By 1860, the widely read New York newspaper, *Harper's Weekly,* was advertising cartridge revolvers and breech-loading rifles for sale at $45 each. Owning such new weapons made wild-game hunting easier, defense against Indians on the still-expanding Western Frontiers more certain, and the Civil War a more deadly conflict.

No area of American life was untouched by water- or steam-driven machines. Farmers were especially favored. A mechanical churn and a cream separator were invented. In 1803, a new corn-shelling machine was shown to President Jefferson by its maker, the Reverend Manasseh Cutler, who wrote of the occasion:

> *The President mounted the carriage—examined the machine—and insisted on turning the crank himself—which he did—and made it go like a whirligig. To his great astonishment the cobs came out as fast as they could fly out at the opening—perfectly whole and clean of the corn. The shelled corn fell below, entirely clean, as if it had been winnowed.*

A mechanical horse-rake of 1856.

Thereafter, machines which were to change the whole pattern of farm life came thick and fast. New plows, planters or sowing machines, and cultivators made the age-old work of farming less backbreaking. Wider, stronger, steel (instead of wooden) plows could turn several furrows at once. One man and two horses could now do in a few hours what would previously have taken several days.

The most revolutionary farm machine was the reaper, patented by Cyrus McCormick in 1834. His first attempt was a clumsy contrivance with a wheel of revolving knives that cut a field of wheat according to the same principles used by modern machines. The young inventor (he was only twenty-two) foresaw that the vast prairies of the Middle West would soon be the granary of America. So he built his farm implement factory in the new little city of Chicago. The success of his sturdy reaping machine was almost immediate. By 1848, he had made and sold the first hundred. One reason for his rapid success was that he sent agents throughout the countryside to display the reaper and then sell it on the installment plan. Few farmers could resist either the new labor-saving device or the new credit-buying plan.

During the American Revolution the iron mines at Mt. Riga, Connecticut, had supplied ore to hand forges that were making muskets and rifles, ship anchors and chains. Now these same mines fed factories manufacturing kitchen cutlery, the new iron stoves that were rapidly replacing fireplace cooking, and steam-operated reaping and threshing machines. Now at last farm wagon and buggy had springs underneath their hard wooden seats, meaning fewer aching bones after a long ride to town.

Oddly enough, there were springs in carriages before springs under mattresses. There is a story that in 1855 a Mr. Liddy of Watertown, New York, grew tired of waiting for his wife to finish her shopping. He stretched out on the carriage seat and had such a pleasant nap on the spring-filled cushions that he resolved to put springs under his bed, too. Soon after, the first bedspring was made in the carriage shop where he worked.

So eagerly did business men invest their money in the new factories that American's foreign trade expanded explosively. For instance, carriages whose parts had been cut out by machine, then assembled by hand, became known around the civilized world as superior to any others. Soon American carriages of handsome design were being shipped abroad to Cuban and South American markets.

Other inventions helped change the American way of life: for example, the gas lighting put on lamp posts along the streets of Boston in 1822. Country folk came year after year to stare and wonder. What a contrast to the age-old midnight black of city streets, lighted only sporadically by the watchman's lantern.

Canalboats, sturdily built to protect them from buffeting, carry the bulk of the nation's inland trade.

In 1851 the Flying Cloud, *shown fully rigged, was the longest and largest clipper ship in the world.*

Perhaps the greatest blessing of all was the discovery of anesthesia, a word meaning "loss of feeling." Opium had been used by doctors for centuries to deaden pain—sometimes with tragic effect. It was not until 1844 that a Boston dentist successfully used ether and a Scotch physician used chlorophorm to induce sleep before an operation. At last it was possible to have tonsils or appendix removed, not to speak of more serious operations, without facing an ordeal of unbearable pain.

Whalers and Clipper Ships

The whale-oil lamp for home lighting was another innovation. Not until the nineteenth century was it discovered that encasing a flame with glass

Women tend a cylinder printing press.

would make that flame burn more brightly and steadily. At first the glass chimney was placed over a candle, then over a wick set in oil. The whale-oil lamp was a blessing to people who for generations had spent their evenings knitting, reading, and mending clothes and equipment by the flickering light of candle or fire. The new demand for whale oil sent New England's sailing vessels to sea in search of the monster of the deep with its precious oil. The whale also provided a soft, white inflammable substance called *spermaceti,* for candles, and flexible whalebones for milady's corsets. In 1845, the United States had over seven hundred whaling ships at sea. Some voyages lasted as long as three or four years. No wonder the homes of most New England sea captains were built with look-out posts or "widow's walks" on their roof tops. Many a woman must have stood there, straining her eyes seaward, day after day, looking for a sail.

But whaling held an unmatched kind of excitement for seafaring men. Even if there had not been the promise of riches in the trade, to such men the thrilling shout of "Thar she blows!" when a whale was sighted from aloft made discomforts and boredom seem worthwhile.

The whaling industry opened a whole new way of life for farm and city boys who longed for adventure on the high seas. No more signing up for an endless seven years of apprenticeship to a joiner or a blacksmith; no more the daily drudgery of farm chores. Other youths came from families whose fathers and grandfathers had been fishermen. There were many such men in New England, where the soil had always discouraged

Erecting telegraph lines through the canyons of the Sierra Nevada was quite a feat.

WARREN

farming, but where the sea had offered a rich and ready harvest market of cod and halibut, swordfish and sardines. Now from towns like Gloucester, New Bedford, and Nantucket, fishermen's sons signed for long voyages on clipper ships.

Few boys foresaw the loathsome sanitary conditions of the great vessels, the monotony of the salt beef and dry biscuit diet, the overcrowding of the common seaman's quarters below deck, the terror of scrambling up the rigging of a ship in a high gale—or the sting of the whiplash if they complained. But it was certainly exciting. Those boys who tried it came home grown men, matured by hard experience, with a rolling gait that landlocked boys might well admire and envy. Other youths signed up for ships bound for the Orient and the China Trade. These were to bring back cargoes of precious tea for the markets of Eastern cities. They also brought back fragile china, embroidered silks, jade ornaments, and carved teakwood chests to adorn the stately homes of many a Yankee sea captain.

$1. **Whiskers.** $1.

For One Dollar I will send, sealed and postpaid, the "Grecian Compound," highly perfumed, which I warrant to force a heavy growth of hair upon the smoothest face in 5 weeks, or upon bald heads in 8 weeks, without stain or injury to the skin. Entire satisfaction given, or money refunded. Descriptive Circulars mailed free. Address F. L. SHULTZ, P. O. Box 216, Lansingburg, N. Y.

Mail-order advertisements appealed to the vanity of men and women alike.

These majestic three- and four-masted ships, constructed in New England, were long in proportion to their width, with great sails and concave bows. Every part of them was native American: "hardwoods for stout hulls, tall trees for masts, pitch for caulking, hemp for ropes." They were swifter than any ships had ever been. The famous *Sea Witch* in 1850 set sail from New York, rounded Cape Horn, and reached San Francisco Bay's Golden Gate in just ninety-seven days. It was a record voyage, but within a year the *Surprise* and the *Flying Cloud* had cut the record to 89 days.

Because San Francisco was a Gold Rush city in need of every known Eastern product, the clipper ships did a rousing business in transporting food, clothing, building equipment, and furniture, to California. This was much faster and cheaper than sending such loads by Conestoga wagon over the Oregon or Sante Fe Trails. From San Francisco the ships proceeded in ballast to China, where they picked up precious cargoes of Oriental goods for Eastern cities. For a while Yankee-built ships ruled the commerce of the high seas. However, the discovery of natural oil and the first shots of the Civil War turned America's attention landward. Also, British shipbuilders had better iron and steel. Before long, England had regained her old supremacy in ship building and in sea trade.

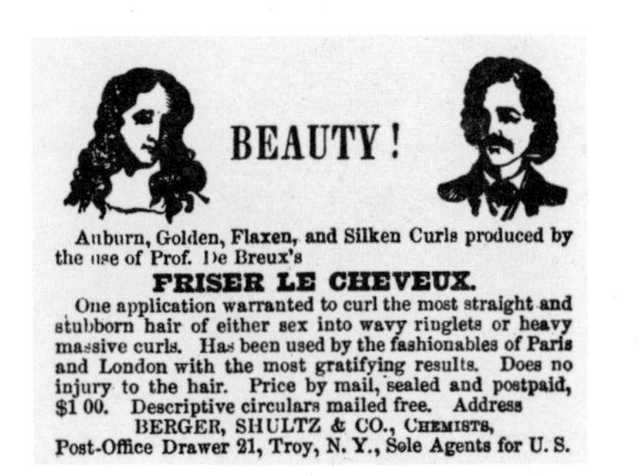

Of course, some lads found themselves signed up on vessels engaged in the ugly slave trade. Though Congress had put a legal stop to the importation of slaves in 1808, thousands continued to be brought from Africa in the dark holds of Yankee ships. For years whole Negro families, even tribes, were smuggled into the ports of Charleston, South Carolina, and other Southern cities, and there sold to tobacco and cotton planters.

New Ways to Spread News

Until the early 1800's the printing presses of America were hand-operated and extremely slow. Now the revolving cylinder press, powered by steam,

Country folk gaze in awe at new-style advertising on New York's Broadway.

made possible the high-speed printing of large city newspapers. Gradually papers that had consisted of a single folded sheet added extra pages. Bit by bit, city newspapers that had been weeklies became dailies. But it still took many weeks for a New York, Philadelphia or Boston paper to find its way overland or by sea to California. One enterprising young "sharpie" paid his ship passage to San Francisco by packing 1500 copies of a New York paper in his trunk. Once out West he sold them to news-hungry settlers for one dollar each.

Until the invention of the daguerreotype in 1839, newspapers, books, and magazines were illustrated by hand-engraved pictures. Because this was a slow, costly process, newspapers, if illustrated at all, met the expense by printing more advertisements than news. Magazines often employed artists to hand-tint prints of steel engravings with watercolor— as in the fashion plates of Godey's *Lady's Magazine.* The growth of photography gradually made it possible to illustrate books in the new way.

The expense of illustration was one reason so few illustrated books were published in nineteenth-century America. Only the Noah Webster Spelling Book and the McGuffey Readers were exceptions. Their enormous popularity evidently warranted a few engraved pictures, like those of the wicked boy in his neighbor's apple tree and "Little Mary at the Churn."

Webster's "Blue-Blacked Speller" had sold over five million copies by 1817, at seven cents each.

Thanks to the new presses and faster distribution, new magazines began to appear. Until mid-nineteenth century American families had had few periodicals. An almanac, which supplied weather predictions, planting times and moral mottoes, had long been accepted as a necessary part of life. So, too, had a few religious tracts and paper-covered sermons. But none of these were real magazines. Now there was a brave new *Atlantic Monthly,* which printed stories, poems, and essays by both American and British writers.

Far-reaching in its effect on communication was the telegraph, a word which means "to write afar off." Its invention was like a miracle. Almost as quickly as thought, man could now send a greeting to his brother many miles away. Telegraph workers suffered the same difficulties as the pioneer: extremes of weather, broad rivers and high mountains, wild animals and Indians. Wires were cut by vandals and childishly curious Indians. Hastily erected poles were blown down by wind and heaved by frost. But each break was repaired, for the telegraph line was a vital link in a truly United States of America.

Settlers in the Far West no longer felt cut off from families and old friends, from political happenings, business trends, or rumors of war. It was no longer necessary to wait for the arrival of a stale Eastern newspaper. Whether the news report was good or bad, news flashed by wire was at least fresh.

Household gadget, 1860.

Won't You Try My Wares?

The new machine-made products poured from the factories: plows, hats, hoopskirts, cookstoves, shaving soap, clocks, and calico. Somehow the American public must be told of these exciting new things that its dollars might buy. Thus was advertising born.

Shouting the praise of what one had to sell was of course not a new idea. The muffin and oyster sellers had long been doing this on street corners with their "Come ye! Come ye! Buy my muffins!" and "Oysters! Oysters! Hot in the shell!" But until the 1800's there had been few ready-made things to sell. Now it was time to persuade people that they no longer needed to buy furniture, dresses, slippers, and toys from abroad. Those made right here in America were just as good—even better!

Among the signs of commercial advertising which fascinated a visitor to New York were the sandwich men, and the wagons with huge signs painted on their sides. In the 1860's in national weeklies we come across advertisements for cosmetics appealing to women's vanity. Often the

Traveling in gaily-painted wagons, medicine men used trumpets and all kinds of hoopla in selling their "miraculous" patent medicines.

HAMLIN'S
WIZARD OIL

THE GREAT MEDICAL WONDER.

There is no Sore it will Not Heal, No Pain it will not Subdue.

HAMLIN'S COUGH BALSAM

PLEASANT TO TAKE

MAGICAL IN ITS EFFECTS.

HAMLIN'S
BLOOD AND LIVER PILLS

For Liver Complaint, Constipation,

AND ALL

Disorders of the Stomach and Digestive Organs.

PREPARED AT THE LABORATORY OF

HAMLINS WIZARD OIL COMPANY, CHICAGO, ILL.

products had never before been offered openly to the public. In 1862, the following appeared in *Harper's Weekly:*

> *BEAUTY—Hunt's Bloom of Roses, a charming and perfectly natural color for the cheeks, or lips. Will not wash off, but remains durable for years. Can only be removed with vinegar, and warranted not to injure the skin. Used by celebrated Court Beauties of Europe exclusively. Mailed free from observation for one dollar.*

Men, too, were easy prey for the new beautifiers. They seemed most responsive to hair-growing concoctions for the face. An advertisement in *Frank Leslie's Weekly* in 1860 announced:

> *Do you want luxuriant whiskers or mustaches? My Onguent will force them to grow heavily in six weeks (upon the smoothest face) without stain or injury to the skin. Price one dollar.*

Mr. Otis demonstrates his remarkable elevator to an astonished crowd.

Women in the government mint in Philadelphia weigh and file metal pieces to be made into coins.

Side by side with the advertisement for Crandall's Patent Spring Rocking Horse with "Health and Happiness in the Same Saddle" and Ballard's Patent Breech-Loading Rifle, there usually appeared the printed praises of a patent medicine or two; for this was the heyday of the cure-all to be found in a single box or bottle for one dollar. Advertisers had learned much from Phineas T. Barnum and had learned it well.

It is easy to understand the great popularity of patent medicines at this time. Doctors were few, and diseases were baffling and many. Besides, thousands of families were setting out for the Far West where they might not be able to find any doctor at all. If the extravagant advertisements seen everywhere—in newspapers, on the sides of barns, and on the face of cliffs—were even partly true, buying a bottle of evil-tasting stuff or a box of green pills was a good investment—a kind of family health insurance.

The Machine Takes its Toll

By mid-nineteenth century every aspect of American life had been changed by the machine, but not always for the better. For the machine

Eager to start life afresh, immigrants arrive from the Old Country.

was exacting a staggering human toll. The new cotton mill, for example, had indeed freed girls from the tyranny of the fireside spinning wheel and supplied even the poorest of them with pretty, cheap calico cloth for their dresses. But by going to work in the new factories they had really exchanged one kind of tyranny for another. Their afterwork hours were spent in dormitories under the strictest supervision, and there were all too few such hours. The "Rules and Regulations to be observed by all persons employed in the factory of AMASA WHITNEY" in 1830 stated as Rule 1:

> *The Mill will be put in operation 10 minutes before sunrise at all seasons of the year. The gate will be shut 10 minutes past sunset from the 20th of March to the 20th of September, at 30 minutes past 8 from the 20th of September to the 20th of March. Saturdays at sunset.*

On the average, the girls worked about seventy hours each week, and for shockingly little pay.

Harriet Martineau, an English visitor to New England's factory towns, recorded the sad fact that children sat beside their older sisters at the long work benches, and earned only one dollar a week for their efforts. Miss Martineau did not seem shocked at this fact. In her own country, too, child labor was not unusual at this time.

More and more poverty-stricken parents were enticed into feeding the machine's insatiable appetite with the labor of their children. So it was that, instead of attending school, thousands of boys and girls spent the bright hours of every working day at canning tables, in the pitheads of mines or in front of blazing furnaces. Others bent over cotton rows under the broiling Southern sun. These children filled, then dragged along the ground, great sacks heavy with the white harvest. Such field work was necessary if the machines were to be kept whirring.

Poverty and overcrowding soon turned many city districts into slums.

Waves of Immigrants

There were not enough workers to satisfy the demands of the machine, dig the canals, lay the rails, and set the telegraph poles. Across the Atlantic there were thousands of Germans, Irish, and Englishmen, eager to immigrate to America—the land of promise. Across the Pacific there were Chinese with the same desire. Some of the immigrants were hungry, for in 1846 there was a terrible potato famine in Ireland. Many were land-hungry people who had for generations dreamed of some day owning the earth they tilled. America's unfenced West with its cheap land looked like the answer to this dream. Others were tired of farming and hoped for new and exciting city jobs.

So they came, a trickle of them in the 1820's—increasing in number until the trickle became a tidal wave. After an ocean crossing of a month to six weeks in the crowded holds of great ships, most of the immigrants

arrived in New York or San Francisco with empty pockets. But almost all shared a powerful urge to "get ahead." By 1850, of the twenty-three million people then in the United States, nearly a million had recently come from Ireland, half a million from Germany and a goodly number from Austria and Hungary, Bohemia, and the Scandinavian countries.

Some of the newcomers manned machines in the factories. Some took domestic service. Now that it was possible to hire a cook, maid, or even a butler, people of means in Northern cities were at last able to maintain their homes and entertain in what they considered to be a sophisticated European manner. Other immigrants went west.

Charles Dickens described in his *American Notes* two young newcomers to New York whom he observed on Broadway:

> *Irishmen both! You might know them if they were masked, by their long-tailed blue coats and bright buttons and their drab trousers, which they wore like men well used to working dresses, who are easy in no others. It would be hard to keep your model republics going without the countrymen and countrywomen of these two laborers. For who else would dig, and delve, and drudge, and do domestic work, and make canals, and roads, and execute lines of Internal Improvement!*

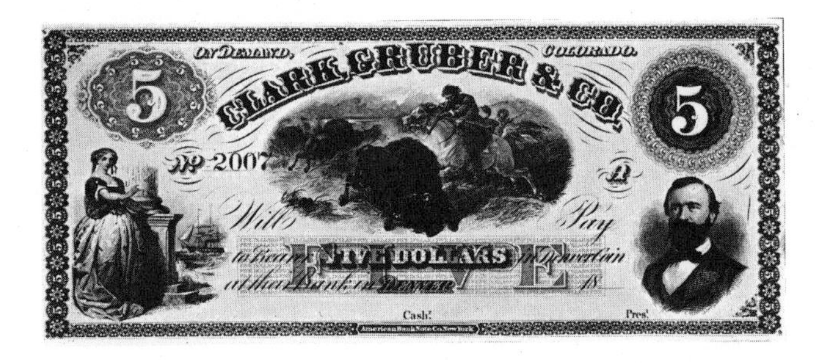

The great influx changed the whole face of American life, especially in the cities. There were difficulties, of course. Cities grew faster than they could absorb their new residents, and slum areas increased frighteningly. Sometimes, too, there were street fights between native American factory workers (who feared their jobs might be endangered) and the newcomers. There were outbursts of religious intolerance. For America had thus far been largely Protestant; now there were many Roman Catholics and Jews whose beliefs and ways of life were not understood. And with the Chinese there was a new color of skin to grow accustomed to. It meant that long working hours and poor pay for factory jobs grew worse rather than better. Machines had multiplied too fast for Congress to control their uses by law. There was need for legislation about working conditions, safety measures, child labor. All of this would come in time.

The First Millionaires

At the turn of the century, most merchants and craftsmen were in business only for themselves. These men were perfectly willing to barter their goods for whatever product the buyer offered. Hand-crafted pewter platters or windowpanes for a new house might be exchanged for maple syrup, firewood, or a new roof on a barn. One reason for this was that America in 1800 had so little actual money in circulation. The paper money printed by the Congress and even by individual banks in the early years after the Revolution was still not entirely trusted by many people. Some "pine tree shillings" had been minted in Vermont as a protest against British coins. But there was still more English money than American in circulation.

Before long, it dawned upon a few clever men in the Eastern cities that if one had some money to begin with, he need not earn his living, as the Bible said, by the "sweat of his brow." Simply by investing his money in someone else's business, he might instead sit back and watch his investment accumulate, or if he had misjudged, be swept away. So was born the Stock Exchange on Wall Street in New York City. By means of it, money was poured into projects such as the building of the new canals. These for a time flourished and richly repaid their investors; but the railroad soon

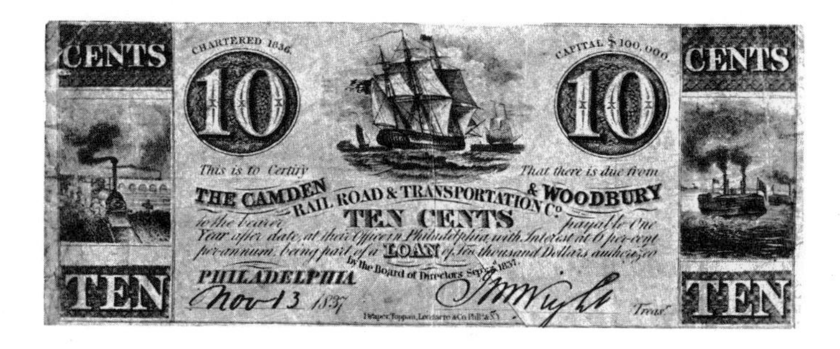

In the 1800's many private banks and other institutions were licensed to print money.

took the canal's place as the best way to travel or to ship one's produce. Much wiser, or perhaps just more lucky, were those who invested in railroads, steamboats, spinning mills—or, later, the firearms factories that manufactured rifles and cannons for the Civil War.

Great fortunes were made or lost in a short time. One such was that of John Jacob Astor who had established stations throughout the Northwest to which wilderness trappers annually brought their beaver, fox, and mink pelts for sale. By "buying out" all competitors, he became the fur king, one of the first men in the nation to establish a business monopoly. He was referred to as a "self-invented money-making machine."

Exaggerated speculation, or venturing large sums of money at high risk in the hope of making enormous profit, sometimes led to disaster. This was especially true during the Civil War, when greedy men pitted their private fortunes, and the labor of many workmen, against the possibility of victory or defeat in the military struggle—gain, not patriotic fervor, was the motive. Because there were no laws to control this system, the country suffered several financial panics during these years. In the first of such shattering "depressions"—caused by a land panic on the Western Frontier in 1819—thousands of pioneer families lost their claim to their partially cleared farms, and the nation's new paper-money system collapsed for a time.

Plight of the Poor

In time the most ignorant laborer knew that the American dream of "equal opportunity for all" was somehow not coming true for everyone. It was obvious that a few men were becoming enormously rich, while the vast majority of workers in the new factories were bending over their machines for fourteen and sixteen hours a day, and for appallingly low wages. So mutterings about the plight of the poor workingman began to be heard in the land. After all, hadn't these men and girls broken away from their home farms or home country in the hope of something better? They began to exert their influence through politics, many casting their votes only for the leader who promised them help.

Early forms of what we now call Labor Unions were established. The "Workie Party" in 1829 elected the president of the Carpenters' Union to the New York State Assembly. It demanded such "radical" changes as a ten-hour day for factory workers, no more imprisonment for debt, and better schools for children. And in 1860, the lady workers of a shoe factory in Lynn, Massachusetts, went on strike. They marched, in street-length gowns and under parasols, through a snowfall, in protest against poor working conditions and low pay. Such were the faint first rumblings of the drive for a more equal distribution of America's wealth and opportunity.

Index

Photographic Credits

(Abbreviations: NYHS New-York Historical Society; NYPL New York Public Library)

p. 7 Gleason's Pictorial, Nov. 29, 1851, NYHS; p. 12 Gun Museum, New Haven; p. 13 Ballou's Pictorial, Jan. 22, 1859, NYHS; p. 14 A. Delano's "Life on the Plains", 1854, NYHS; p. 15 Western Union Telegraph Company; p. 18 A. Delano's *Life on the Plains,* 1854, NYHS; p. 19 (top) Gun Museum, New Haven; p. 19 (bottom) Museum of the Fur Trade, Chadron, Nebraska; p. 20 Ballou's Pictorial, Jan. 7, 1859, NYHS; p. 21 Gleason's Pictorial, March 19, 1853, NYHS; p. 22 Frank Leslie's Illustrated Newspaper, June 3, 1871, NYHS; p. 23 Gleason's Pictorial, March 27, 1852, NYHS; p. 25 Gleason's Pictorial, July 12, 1851, NYHS; p. 26 Ballou's Pictorial, May 3, 1856, NYHS; p. 34 Library of Congress; p. 35 Gleason's Pictorial, Nov. 6, 1852, NYHS; p. 37 Library of Congress; p. 38 Godey's Lady's Book, 1842, NYPL; p. 39 Godey's Lady's Book, 1851, NYPL; p. 42 Courtesy of The New-York Historical Society; p. 43 Library of Congress; p. 44 Abby Aldrich Rockefeller Folk Art Collection; pp. 48–49 Missouri Historical Society; p. 50 Frank Leslie's Illustrated Newspaper, Nov. 22, 1856, NYHS; p. 54 Brown Brothers, New York; p. 55 Ballou's Pictorial, Oct. 20, 1855, NYHS; p. 56 Harper's Weekly, Nov. 2, 1867, Library of Congress; p. 57 New York Central System; pp. 58–59 Courtesy of the Cooper Union Museum (photograph Courtesy of the Museum of the City of New York); Harper's Weekly, May 22, 1858, NYHS; p. 63 Courtesy of The New-York Historical Society; p. 65 Harper's Weekly, Nov. 26, 1859, NYHS; p. 68 East Hampton Historical Society (photograph Courtesy of The New-York Historical Society); pp. 66–67 Harper's Weekly, Nov. 13, 1858; p. 70 Godey's Lady's Book, NYPL; p. 71 The New-York Historical Society Collection; pp. 72–73 Ballou's Pictorial, July 9, 1859, NYHS; p. 74 Ballou's Pictorial, Feb. 23, 1856, NYHS; p. 75 Gleason's Pictorial, Jan. 24, 1852, NYHS; p. 76 Historical Society of York County; p. 77 Metropolitan Museum of Art, Rogers Fund, 1942; p. 78 Gleason's Pictorial, June 28, 1851, NYHS; p. 79 Ballou's Pictorial, July 1856, NYHS; p. 80 Museum of the City of New York; p. 81 Gleason's Pictorial, June 18, 1853, NYHS; p. 82 (top) Frank Leslie's Illustrated Newspaper, Sep. 20, 1856, NYHS; p. 82 (bottom) and p. 83 Godey's Lady's Book, 1864, NYPL; p. 84 Harper's Weekly, Dec. 7, 1867, NYHS; p. 85 (top) Godey's Lady's Book, May 1849, NYHS; p. 85 (bottom) New York Mechanic, May 1, 1841, NYHS; p. 86 Godey's Lady's Book, 1845, NYPL; p. 90 NYHS; p. 91 Museum of the Fur Trade, Chadron, Nebraska; pp. 92–93 Museum of the City of New York; p. 94 NYHS; p. 95 Benjamin Butterworth's *The Growth of Industrial Art,* NYHS; p. 96 NYHS; p. 97 (top) Godey's Lady's Book, 1831, NYPL; p. 97 (bottom) Godey's Lady's Book, 1858, NYPL; p. 100 Ballou's Pictorial, June 13, 1857, NYPL; p. 102 Harper's Weekly, March 23, 1867, NYHS; p. 103 Harper's Weekly, May 14, 1870, NYHS; p. 104 Ballou's Pictorial, July 9, 1859, NYHS; p. 105 Ballou's Pictorial, Sep. 12, 1857, NYPL; p. 106 (top) Gleason's Pictorial, Sep. 11, 1852, NYHS; p. 106 (bottom) Harper's Weekly, Feb. 26, 1859, NYHS; p. 107 (top) Godey's Lady's Book, 1851, NYPL; p. 107 (bottom) Godey's Lady's Book, 1848, NYPL; p. 108 Gleason's Pictorial, Jan. 22, 1853, NYHS; p. 109 Ballou's Pictorial, 1859, NYHS; p. 110 Scientific American, July 9, 1859, NYHS; p. 111 Chicago Historical Society; p. 112 Gleason's Pictorial, Jan. 7, 1854, NYHS; p. 116 Harper's Weekly, March 17, 1866, NYHS; p. 117 Godey's Lady's Book, 1842, NYPL; p. 119 Godey's Lady's Book, 1860, NYPL; pp. 120–121 Godey's Lady's Book, 1853, NYPL; pp. 122–123 Historical Society of York County; pp. 124–125 Harper's Weekly, May 18, 1867, NYHS; p. 126 Harper's Weekly, Sep. 12, 1874, NYHS; p. 128 NYHS; p. 129 Metropolitan Museum of Art, Rogers Fund, 1942; p. 131 Ballou's Pictorial, July 23, 1859, NYHS; p. 134 Historical Society of York County; p. 135 NYHS; p. 137 Metropolitan Museum of Art, Rogers Fund, 1942; pp. 138–139 Gleason's Pictorial, Sep. 18, 1852, NYHS; p. 140 Metropolitan Museum of Art, Rogers Fund, 1942; p. 141 Godey's Lady's Book, 1868, NYPL; p. 143 Harper's Weekly, Feb. 19, 1859, NYHS; p. 144 Harper's Weekly, Jan. 29, 1859, NYHS; p. 145 Singer Sewing Machine Co.; pp. 146–147 Hat Corporation of America; p. 149 Museum Colt Collection, Connecticut State Library, Hartford; p. 150 Chicago Historical Society; p. 151 Benjamin Butterworth's *The Growth of Industrial Art,* NYHS; p. 152 Gleason's Pictorial, Dec. 25, 1852, NYHS; p. 153 Gleason's Pictorial, May 31, 1851, NYHS; p. 154 Gleason's Pictorial, Nov. 22, 1851, NYHS; p. 155 Western Union Telegraph Company; p. 156 Harper's Weekly, Aug. 26, 1865, NYHS; p. 157 Harper's Weekly, Jan. 18, 1868, NYHS; p. 158 Harper's Weekly, Sep. 8, 1860, NYHS; p. 159 Bella C. Landauer Collection, NYHS; p. 160 Otis Elevator Company; p. 161 Gleason's Pictorial, July 17, 1852, NYHS; pp. 162–163 Museum of the City of New York; pp. 166–167 The Chase Manhattan Bank Money Museum.

DESIGNED BY ULRICH RUCHTI